# ESSENTIALS FOR LIVING

## HOMEWORK ASSIGNMENTS BOOK

**Eilis Flood**

Gill & Macmillan

Gill & Macmillan Ltd
Hume Avenue
Park West
Dublin 12
with associated companies throughout the world
www.gillmacmillan.ie


© Eilis Flood 2010
978 0 7171 46703
Design and typesetting by Design Image, Dublin
Artwork by ODI, Oxford

*The paper used in this book is made from the wood pulp of managed forests. For every tree felled, at least one tree is planted, thereby renewing natural resources.*

# Contents

## Unit 1 Food

**Chapter 1**

Homework Assignment 1: Introduction to Nutrition and Protein     2

Homework Assignment 2: Fats     5

Homework Assignment 3: Carbohydrates     7

Homework Assignment 4: Vitamins     10

Homework Assignment 5: Minerals     13

Homework Assignment 6: Energy and Water     15

**Chapter 2**

Homework Assignment 7: The Digestive System     17

**Chapter 3**

Homework Assignment 8: A Balanced Diet     19

**Chapter 4**

Homework Assignment 9: Special Diets     25

**Chapter 5**

Homework Assignment 10: Meal Planning     31

**Chapter 6**

Homework Assignment 11: Good Food Hygiene and Storage     34

**Chapter 7**

Homework Assignment 12: Preparing to Cook     37

**Chapter 8**

Homework Assignment 13: Cooking Food     40

## Chapter 10

Homework Assignment 14: Meat and Meat Alternatives                43

Homework Assignment 15: Poultry                                   47

Homework Assignment 16: Fish                                      49

Homework Assignment 17: Eggs                                      54

Homework Assignment 18: Milk and Yoghurt                          57

Homework Assignment 19: Cheese                                    61

Homework Assignment 20: Cereals and Potatoes                      64

Homework Assignment 21: Fruit                                     69

Homework Assignment 22: Vegetables                                72

Homework Assignment 23: Combination Foods                         77

## Chapter 11

Homework Assignment 24: Breakfasts and Packed Meals               80

Homework Assignment 25: Soups                                     85

Homework Assignment 26: Sauces, Herbs and Spices                  91

## Chapter 12

Homework Assignment 27: Food Processing and Leftovers             95

## Chapter 13

Homework Assignment 28: Home Baking                               100

## Unit 2 Consumer studies

## Chapter 15

Homework Assignment 29: Consumers and Shopping                    104

## Chapter 16

Homework Assignment 30: Advertising                               109

## Chapter 17

Homework Assignment 31: Consumer Protection and Making a Complaint  111

**Chapter 18**

Homework Assignment 32: Quality     115

**Chapter 19**

Homework Assignment 33: Money Management     118

## Unit 3 Social studies

**Chapter 20**

Homework Assignment 34: The Family     122

**Chapter 21**

Homework Assignment 35: Growth and Development     125

**Chapter 22**

Homework Assignment 36: New Life     128

**Chapter 23**

Homework Assignment 37: The Human Body – The Teeth     132
Homework Assignment 38: The Human Body – The Skin and Personal Hygiene     135
Homework Assignment 39: The Human Body – Respiratory System     139
Homework Assignment 40: The Human Body – The Circulatory System     141

**Chapter 24**

Homework Assignment 41: Health Education     144

## Unit 4 Resource management and home studies

**Chapter 25**

Homework Assignment 42: Home Management     150

**Chapter 26**

Homework Assignment 43: Home Design and Room Planning     151

**Chapter 27**

Homework Assignment 44: Services to the Home 156

**Chapter 28**

Homework Assignment 45: Technology in the Home 161

**Chapter 29**

Homework Assignment 46: Home Hygiene, Safety and First Aid 167

**Chapter 30**

Homework Assignment 47: Community Services and the Environment 172

## Unit 5 Textile studies

**Chapter 31**

Homework Assignment 48: Textiles in the Home 178

**Chapter 32**

Homework Assignment 49: Clothing, Fashion and Design 181

**Chapter 33**

Homework Assignment 50: Fibres and Fabrics 183

**Chapter 34**

Homework Assignment 51: Fabric Care 191

**Chapter 35**

Homework Assignment 52: Needlework Skills 195

**Chapter 36**

Homework Assignment 53: Practical Needlework Tasks 199

## eTest.ie – what is it?

A revolutionary new website-based testing platform that facilitates a social learning environment for Irish schools. Both students and teachers can use it, either independently or together, to make the whole area of testing easier, more engaging and more productive for all.

## Students – do you want to know how well you are doing? Then take an eTest!

At eTest.ie, you can access tests put together by the author of this textbook. You get instant results, so they're a brilliant way to quickly check just how your study or revision is going.

Since each eTest is based on your textbook, if you don't know an answer, you'll find it in your book.

Register now and you can save all of your eTest results to use as a handy revision aid or to simply compare with your friends' results!

## Teachers – eTest.ie will engage your students and help them with their revision, while making the jobs of reviewing their progress and homework easier and more convenient for all of you.

Register now to avail of these exciting features:

- Create tests easily using our pre-set questions OR you can create your own questions

- Develop your own online learning centre for each class that you teach

- Keep track of your students' performances

eTest.ie has a wide choice of question types for you to choose from, most of which can be graded automatically, like multiple-choice, jumbled-sentence, matching, ordering and gap-fill exercises. This free resource allows you to create class groups, delivering all the functionality of a VLE (Virtual Learning Environment) with the ease of communication that is brought by social networking.

# Unit 1
# Food

Date of issue                                           Due date

**HL 2007, 2004, 2003, 1998**

**OL 2004**

**Introduction to nutrition**

1. List the three functions of food in the body.

   (i) _Heat and energy_

   (ii) _Growth and repair_

   (iii) _Helps fight disease_

   | 3 |

2. Describe the three ways an individual may be malnourished.

   (i) _Too little of ceartain foods_

   (ii) _Too much of certain foods_

   (iii) _Too little food_

   | 3 |

3. All foods contain one or more of the six nutrients. Name the six nutrients.

   (i) _Protein_    (ii) _Corbohydrats_    (iii) _Vitamins_

   (iv) _Fat_    (v) _Water_    (vi) _Minerals_

   | 6 |

4. What is the difference (differentiate) between macronutrients and micronutrients?

   _Macronutrients must be broken down by the body while micronutrient need no digestion_

   | 4 |

5. Name two nutrients under each of the following headings.

   (i)  Macronutrients:

     (a) protein      (b) Fat

   (ii)  Micronutrients:

     (a) Minereals      (b) Vitamins    4

6. Suggest four factors that influence a person's food choices.

   (i) Religion

   (ii) Gost

   (iii) Season

   (iv) what you like    4

## Protein

7. Using a simple diagram, describe the composition of protein.

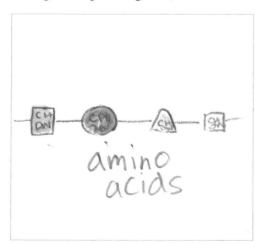

amino acids

Protein is made oS simple amino acids.
Carbon, hydrogen, oxygen & nitrogen ( CHON)    2

8. List four sources of both animal and vegetable protein.

   (i)  Animal protein foods:

     (a) meat (b) Sish (c) cheese (d) milk

   (ii)  Vegetable protein foods:

     (a) Beans (b) Peas (c) rice (d) lentils   8

9. Name four foods that are good sources of high biological value protein.

(i) _____ meat _____ (ii) _____ eggs _____

(iii) _____ milk _____ (iv) _____ Sish _____ | 4 |

10. Meat is a good source of protein. Why is protein important in the diet?

Protein repairs worn out damaged cells, Growth, make | 4 |

11. What do the letters RDA stand for and mean?

Recommended Daily Allowance | 2 |

12. Explain any two of the following: (i) amino acid (ii) high biological value protein (iii) textured vegetable protein or mycoprotein.

High biological value protein food usually meat
Textured Vegtable protein – high in protein and calcium, low in Sat. | 4 |

13. What are the main sources of protein in your diet?

Milk, meat, eggs, cheese | 2 |

Total Mark

**Homework Assignment 1**

| 50 |

*Teacher's comment*

| Chapter 1 | Fats |
|---|---|

Date of issue          Due date

**HL 2006, 1998**

**OL 2008, 2006, 2005, 2000, 1994**

1. Using a simple diagram, describe the composition of fat.

 

|2|

2. Complete the table by placing each of the following foods under the heading that indicates the type of fat present.

cheese, cooking oil, egg yolk, fatty meat, nuts,
oily fish, sausages, whole cereals

| Saturated fat | Unsaturated fat |
|---|---|
| | |

|8|

3.  What are the **four** main functions of fat in the diet?

    (i) Gives us lots of heat and energy.
    A layer of fats under the skin called adipose tissue insulates
    (ii) the body. Chelps keep the body warm.
    Delicate organs such as the heart & kidneys have a layer of fat around
    (iii) them; this layer can protect them from injury.
    Vitamins A,D,E and K dissolve in fat. When we eat fat, we are also
    (iv) eating these vitamins.

    4

4.  Suggest **four** ways of reducing the intake of fat in the diet.

    (i) Grill, bake, boil or microwave food instead of frying.

    (ii) Cut down on foods like crisps, burgers & chips.

    (iii) Cut fat off meat.

    (iv) Use low-fat foods.

    4

5.  What are the main sources of fat in your diet? Are they from saturated or unsaturated sources?

    _____

    _____

    4

Total Mark

**Homework Assignment 2**

22

*Teacher's comment*

_____

| Chapter 1 | Carbohydrates |
| --- | --- |

Date of issue                                        Due date

HL  2009, 2004, 2001, 1997

OL  2008, 2005, 2002, 1999, 1995

1.  Using a simple diagram, describe the composition of carbohydrate.

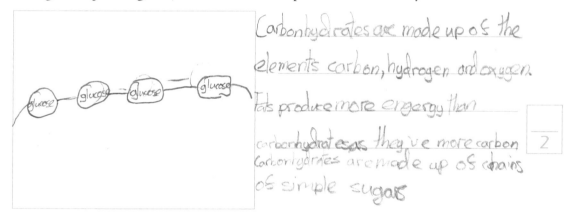

Carbohydrates are made up of the elements carbon, hydrogen and oxygen.

Fats produce more energy than carbohydrates as they've more carbon

Carbohydrates are made up of chains of simple sugars

2

2.  Carbohydrates are classified into three different groups. List five examples of foods under each group.

| Sugars | Starches | Fibre-rich foods |
| --- | --- | --- |
| Honey | Bread | Brown bread |
| biscuits | pasta | Brown rice |
| chocolate | vegetables carrots broccoli | fruits |
| cake | breakfast cereals | vegetables |
| ice-cream | potatoes | fibre-rich breakfastcereals |

3. List three functions of carbohydrates in the diet.

(i) _____

(ii) _____

(iii) _____　　3

4. What is the main function of (reason for including) fibre in the diet?

It helps waste pass easily through the intestines, if we
don't eat enough fibre, we risk constipation & diseases such as　2
bowel cancer.

5. Do you think you eat enough fibre? Explain your answer.

I do not think that I eat enough fibre
because I honestly don't like Brown bread, rice
or pasta and wheatabixs make me sick.　　4

6. Suggest three ways to increase fibre in the diet.

(i) Eat brown bread and rice instead of white

(ii) Eat more fresh fruit and vegetable.

(iii) Eat high-fibre breakfast cereal.　　3

7. What are empty-calorie foods?

They have little goodness, they are high-calorie foods, don't supply any of the　2
other nutrients needed by the body.

8. What (if any) empty-calorie foods do you consume on a regular basis?

Fizzy drinks and sweets　　2

8

9. Examine three products in your presses at home. In the table below, record how much sugar is contained in 100g of the product.

| Name of product | Grams of sugar per 100g of product |
|---|---|
| (i) Caster sugar | 100g |
| (ii) Hellmann's mayonnaise | 1.5g |
| (iii) Colman's mustard | 0.6g |

3

10. Suggest four ways of reducing the intake of sugar in the diet.

(i) _____

(ii) _____

(iii) _____

(iv) _____

4

Total / Mark

**Homework Assignment 3**

*Teacher's comment*

40

Date of issue                                            Due date

**HL  2008, 2002, 2000**

**OL  2009, 2008, 2000**

1.  Name two fat-soluble and two water-soluble vitamins.

    (i)   Fat-soluble vitamins:

        (a) _____    (b) _____

    (ii)  Water-soluble vitamins:

        (a) _____    (b) _____    | 4 |

2.  Give three important sources of each of the following vitamins.

    | Vitamin | Three sources |
    |---|---|
    | (i)    Vitamin C | |
    | (ii)   Vitamin A (pure) | |
    | (iii)  Vitamin D | |
    | (iv)   B group | |

    | 12 |

3.  Name one vitamin required to prevent each of the following
    deficiency diseases.

    | Deficiency disease | Vitamin required |
    |---|---|
    | (i)    Scurvy | |
    | (ii)   Night blindness | |
    | (iii)  Beriberi | |
    | (iv)   Rickets | |

    | 4 |

4. Vitamin C is easily destroyed by careless storage and cooking. Explain five ways to help prevent this loss.

(i) _____

(ii) _____

(iii) _____

(iv) _____

(v) _____

5

5. List one function of each of the following vitamins.

| Vitamin | Function |
|---|---|
| (i) Vitamin C | |
| (ii) B group | |
| (iii) Vitamin A | |
| (iv) Vitamin D | |
| (v) Vitamin K | |

5

6. What is rickets? How can it be prevented?

_____

_____

2

7. What are the two main sources of vitamin C in your diet?

(i) _____ (ii) _____

2

8. Explain **each** of the following.

   (i) Osteoporosis: _____

   _____

   (ii) Hypervitaminosis: _____

   _____

**Homework Assignment 4**

*Teacher's comment*

38

Homework Assignment 5

| Chapter 1 | Minerals |
| --- | --- |

Date of issue                           Due date

HL  2007, 2000, 1999, 1997, 1996, 1995, 1994

OL  2008, 2007, 2005, 2003, 2002, 2001, 2000

1.  List five important minerals needed by the body.

    (i) _____   (ii) _____   (iii) _____

    (iv) _____   (v) _____                    | 5 |

2.  List one important function of each of the following minerals.

    | Mineral | Function |
    | --- | --- |
    | (i)   Iron | |
    | (ii)   Calcium | |
    | (iii)   Iodine | |
    | (iv)   Sodium | |
    | (v)   Fluorine | |
    | (vi)   Phosphorus | |

    | 6 |

3.  Identify one possible health problem associated with each of the
    following dietary habits.

    | Dietary intake | Possible health problems |
    | --- | --- |
    | (i)   Low intake of iron | |
    | (ii)   Low intake of calcium | |
    | (iii)   High intake of salt | |

    | 3 |

4. What are the two main sources of calcium and iron in your diet?

   (i) Calcium:

     (a) _____ (b) _____

   (ii) Iron:

     (a) _____ (b) _____     4

5. Name the vitamins that help the absorption of each of the following minerals. (1999 HL)

| Mineral | Vitamin that helps absorption |
| --- | --- |
| (i)    Calcium | |
| (ii)   Iron | |

2

Total / Mark

**Homework Assignment 5**

20

*Teacher's comment*

**Homework Assignment 6**

| Chapter 1 | Energy and Water |

Date of issue                                    Due date

## HL  2009, 2003, 1997

1. List six good sources of water in the diet.

    (i) _____     (ii) _____

    (iii) _____     (iv) _____

    (v) _____     (vi) _____     `3`

2. Describe three functions of water in the body.

    (i) _____

    (ii) _____

    (iii) _____     `3`

3. List four properties of water.

    (i) _____

    (ii) _____

    (iii) _____

    (iv) _____     `4`

4. Explain the term 'energy balance'.

    _____     `2`

5. List **four** factors that influence an individual's energy requirements.

(i) _____

(ii) _____

(iii) _____

         4

(iv) _____

**Total / Mark**

**Homework Assignment 6**

     16

*Teacher's comment*

## Chapter 2    The Digestive System

Date of issue                                        Due date

**HL    2003, 1997, 1996**

1.  Label the diagram below of the digestive system.

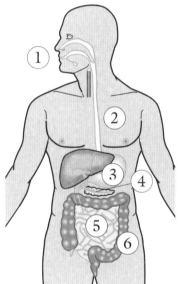

1. _____

2. _____

4. _____

4. _____

5. _____

6. _____        | 6 |

2.  Name the digestive enzyme found in the mouth and give its function.

    _____        | 4 |

3.  Food undergoes many changes before nutrients pass into the bloodstream
    and are transported around the body.
    (i)  Differentiate between the physical and chemical breakdown of food.

        (a)  Physical breakdown of food is: _____

        (b)  Chemical breakdown of food is: _____        | 4 |

    (ii)  Outline one chemical change that occurs in food in the following.

        (a)  The stomach: _____

        (b)  The small intestine: _____        | 4 |

(iii) State the product each of the following nutrients is converted to during digestion.

(a) Protein to: _____

(b) Carbohydrate to: _____

(c) Fat to: _____

3

(iv) Explain why white fish is more digestible than oily fish.

_____

2

4. (i) State the functions of each of the following parts of the digestive system.

(a) The mouth: _____

_____

(b) The stomach: _____

_____

(c) The small intestine: _____

_____

6

(ii) Explain what is meant by peristalsis.

_____

2

(iii) What is the role of fibre in digestion?

_____

2

Total Mark

**Homework Assignment 7**

33

*Teacher's comment*

_____

**Chapter 3     A Balanced Diet**

Date of issue                                    Due date

**HL   2005, 1996**

**OL   1998**

1.   Label the diagram of the food pyramid by writing in the correct food group.

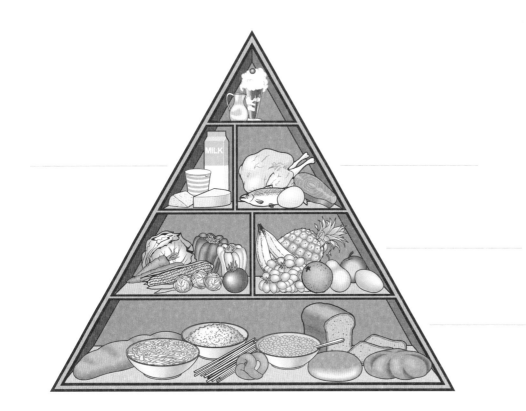

4

2. Complete the table below to show how many servings from each group are required by people of different ages.

| Food group | Age group | Number of servings per day |
|---|---|---|
| Meat group | Breastfeeding mother | |
| Meat group | Teenager | |
| Fruit and vegetable group | Adult | |
| Cereal and potato group | Children | |
| Cereal and potato group | Pregnant woman | |
| Milk group | Teenager | |
| Milk group | Adult | |
| Milk group | Pregnant woman | |

8

3. List four general healthy eating guidelines.

(i) _____

(ii) _____

(iii) _____

(iv) _____

4

4. List five pieces of dietary advice you would give to someone with a new baby.

(i) _____

_____

(ii) _____

_____

(iii) _____

_____

(iv) _____

_____

(v) _____

_____

5

5. Sandra is a lone parent, surviving on welfare payments. She has two young children. While she wants to do the best she can for her children, she does not really know much about nutrition or healthy eating. List five pieces of advice you would give Sandra about feeding her children a balanced diet.

(i) _____

_____

(ii) _____

_____

(iii) _____

_____

(iv) _____

_____

(v) _____

_____

5

6. List three occupations that would be considered sedentary and three that would be considered manual.

(i) Sedentary:

(a) _____ (b) _____ (c) _____

(ii) Manual:

(a) _____ (b) _____ (c) _____

6

7. What should be the main difference between a sedentary and manual worker's diet?

_____ | 2 |

8. Why should a woman take folic acid supplements before and during pregnancy?

_____ | 2 |

9. Jane has just discovered that she is pregnant. Write down four pieces of advice that you would offer her for a healthy diet during pregnancy.

(i) _____

(ii) _____

(iii) _____

(iv) _____ | 4 |

10. Complete the table below to show that you understand why certain dietary guidelines are given to the elderly.

| Dietary guideline | Reason for guideline |
|---|---|
| (i) Choose low-fat cheese, milk and yoghurt | |
| (ii) Limit foods such as butter, sausages, cakes and biscuits | |
| (iii) Eat plenty of fruit and vegetables | |
| (iv) Choose brown bread, rice and pasta instead of white | |
| (v) Limit intakes of highly processed foods | |

| 5 |

11. Below is a hospital lunch menu. Give reasons in the space provided why the menu is suitable for a person recovering from illness.

| Menu | Reasons why menu is suitable |
| --- | --- |
| Chicken broth | |
| Baked fish pie topped with mashed potato | |
| Steamed carrots and broccoli | |
| Stewed apple and custard | |

5

12. **Chicken casserole**

| | |
| --- | --- |
| 1 chicken | 25g oil |
| 2 tomatoes | 1 stick celery (optional) |
| 25g flour | salt and pepper |
| 2 streaky rashers | 100g mushrooms |
| 2 medium onions | 375ml stock |

(i) Examine the ingredients used in this recipe and state, giving reasons, if they concur with current healthy eating guidelines.

_____

_____

_____

_____

_____

4

(ii)  Design a two-course menu for an evening meal in summer, using the chicken casserole as the main dish.

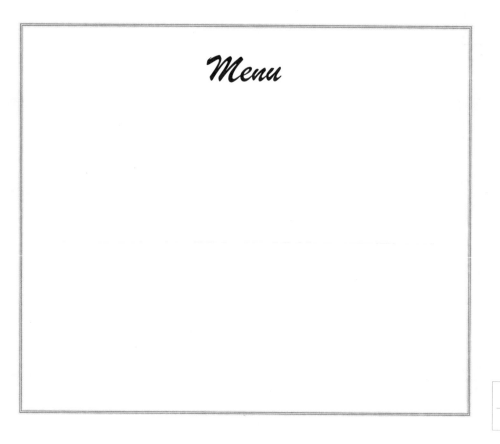

*Menu*

4

13.  Name the food group for each of the foods listed in the table below.

| Food | Food group |
|------|------------|
| Yoghurt | |
| Apples | |
| Rice | |
| Whiting | |

4

Total Mark

**Homework Assignment 8**

62

*Teacher's comment*

**Chapter 4**   Special Diets

Date of issue                                    Due date

**HL**  2009, 2008, 2006, 2004, 2003, 2002, 1996, 1995

**OL**  2009, 2005, 2003 (usually just asked to suggest ways to reduce sugar, fat
and salt and increase fibre)

1.   Vegetarian diets are becoming more popular in Ireland today.
(i)   Give three reasons why people may choose a vegetarian diet.

(a) Healthier diet

(b) Religious reasons

(c) Hormones being pumped into animals     | 3 |

(ii)   Explain each of the following types of vegetarian diets.

(a) Vegan: Strict vegetarian - only eat plant foods

(b) Lactovegetarian: Eat animal products e.g milk, cheese,    | 4 |
soya milk

(iii)   List four guidelines that should be followed when planning meals for
a vegetarian.

(a) Get enough iron

(b) Get enough protein

(c) Get enough fibre

(d) _____     | 4 |

(iv) Design a balanced **three-course** dinner menu suitable for a lactovegetarian.

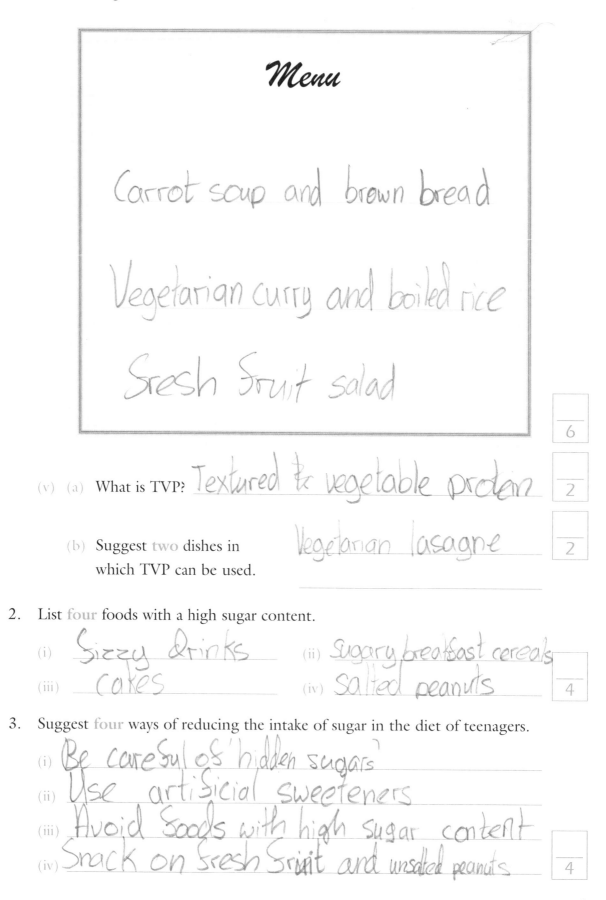

*Menu*

Carrot soup and brown bread

Vegetarian curry and boiled rice

Sresh Sruit salad

6

(v) (a) What is TVP? Textured te vegetable protem

2

(b) Suggest **two** dishes in which TVP can be used.

Vegetarian lasagne

2

2. List **four** foods with a high sugar content.

(i) Sizzy drinks          (ii) Sugary breakfast cereals

(iii) Cakes          (iv) Salted peanuts

4

3. Suggest **four** ways of reducing the intake of sugar in the diet of teenagers.

(i) Be careful of 'hidden sugars'

(ii) Use artificial sweeteners

(iii) Avoid foods with high sugar content

(iv) Snack on fresh Sruit and unsalted peanuts

4

4. Suggest four ways of reducing the intake of fat in the diet.

(i) Eat pleny of fruit and veg

(ii) Use low-fat products.

(iii) Eat fewer foods from the top of the pyramid

(iv) Use Flora

`[4]`

5. (i) State the recommended daily salt intake for an adult.

4-6g

`[2]`

(ii) What effect can a high salt intake have on the body?

To much salt in the diet causes high blood pressure, which can lead to strokes and heart attacks.

`[4]`

(iii) Suggests four ways of reducing salt intake in the diet.

(a) Avoid foods high in salt

(b) Choose fresh meat and veg

(c) Flavour dishes with herbs, spices and pepper

(d) Use soft low-sodium alternatives like LoSalt

`[4]`

6. (i) What is meant by coronary heart disease?

When a fatty substance know as cholesterol blocks an artery a heart attack occurs

`[2]`

(ii) Suggest the guidelines that should be followed to reduce the risk of coronary heart disease.

`[6]`

7. Obesity has become a major health hazard.

   (i) Outline the causes of obesity.

   _____

   _____

   _____

   _____ | 4 |

   (ii) List four health problems associated with obesity.

   (a) _____

   (b) _____

   (c) _____

   (d) _____ | 4 |

   (iii) Suggest four healthy eating guidelines that should be followed to reduce the risk of obesity.

   (a) _____

   (b) _____

   (c) _____

   (d) _____ | 4 |

(iv) Plan out a set of menus for one day suitable for an adult who is obese.

## Menu

### Breakfast

### Lunch

### Dinner

### Snacks

8

(v) Explain the term 'empty calories'.

Provide a lot of

2

8. Diabetes occurs when the body produces too much or too little of a particular chemical. Name this chemical.

2

9. What information does this symbol convey to the consumer?

_____ 2

10. Explain why some foods must be excluded from a coeliac diet.

_____

_____ 3

**Homework Assignment 9**

*Teacher's comment*

80

| Chapter 5 | Meal Planning |
| --- | --- |

Date of issue                              Due date

**HL  2004, 1998, 1999**

**OL   2000**

1.  List six factors that may affect meal planning.

   (i) _____

   (ii) _____

   (iii) _____

   (iv) _____

   (v) _____

   (vi) _____          | 6 |

2.  Explain each of the following terms.

   (i)  Table d'hôte: _____

   _____          | 2 |

   (ii)  À la carte: _____

   _____          | 2 |

3.  What is the purpose of serving an appetiser before a meal?

   _____

   _____          | 2 |

4.  Name a different food for which each of the following garnishes may be suitable.

| Garnish | Food |
| --- | --- |
| (i)   A lemon wedge | |
| (ii)   Chopped parsley | |
| (iii)   Glacé cherries | |
| (iv)   A sprinkle of icing sugar | |

4

5.  (i)   Plan and set out a menu for a two-course main meal, for yourself and three friends, that can be prepared and served in one hour.

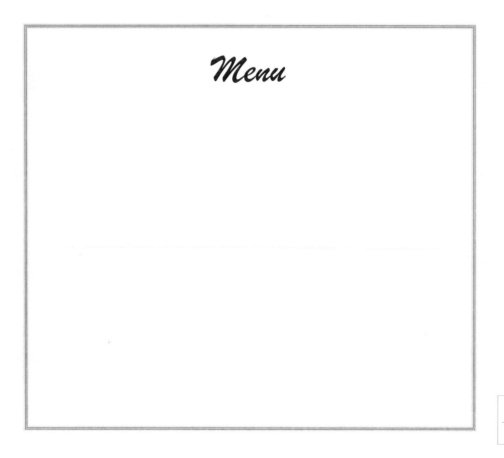

Menu

4

(ii) Evaluate the nutritive value of the meal (see p. 22 in your textbook on the dietary needs of adolescents/teenagers).

_____

_____

_____

_____ | 10 |

6. (i) Suggest two garnishes suitable for fresh vegetable soup. | 2 |

(a) _____ (b) _____

(ii) Plan and set out a three-course dinner menu to include the vegetable soup.

*Menu*

| 6 |

Date of issue                                    Due date

**HL  2008, 2007, 2005, 2000, 1996**

**OL  2000**

1.  List the four main causes of food spoilage and explain five conditions that favour the growth of food spoilage micro-organisms.

   (i)  Causes of food spoilage:

   (a) _____  (b) _____

   (c) _____  (d) _____        | 4 |

   (ii)  Conditions that favour the growth of micro-organisms:

   (a) _____

   (b) _____

   (c) _____

   (d) _____

   (e) _____        | 5 |

2.  (i)  Name one food-poisoning bacteria. _____        | 2 |

   (ii)  Give two possible sources of this bacteria.

   (a) _____  (b) _____        | 4 |

   (iii)  List three symptoms of food poisoning.

   (a) _____  (b) _____

   (c) _____                                        | 3 |

3. Describe four ways food can become infected with food-poisoning bacteria.

   (i) _____

   (ii) _____

   (iii) _____

   (iv) _____  _____ | 4 |

4. (i) What precautions should be taken when buying, storing and cooking 'ready-to-cook' meals to avoid the risk of food poisoning?

   (a) Buying: _____

   _____ | 2 |

   (b) Storing: _____

   _____ | 2 |

   (c) Cooking: _____

   _____ | 2 |

   (ii) Name one food-poisoning bacteria that is associated with poultry.

   _____ | 2 |

5. What do the letters HACCP mean in relation to food hygiene and storage?

   _____ | 2 |

6. Explain each of the following terms displayed on food packaging.

   (i) Best before date: _____ | 2 |

   (ii) Use by date: _____ | 2 |

   (iii) Expiry date: _____ | 2 |

   (iv) Sell by date: _____ | 2 |

7.  Explain the term 'cross-contamination'.

    _____

    _____  | 2 |

8.  Give two example of each of the following.  | 2 |

    (i)   Perishable foods:      (a) _____   (b) _____  | 2 |

    (ii)  Non-perishable foods:  (a) _____   (b) _____  | 2 |

    (iii) Semi-perishable foods  (a) _____   (b) _____  | 2 |

9.  Explain the term 'shelf life'.

    _____  | 2 |

10. Name two different types of packaging in which food can be frozen.

    (i) _____      (ii) _____  | 2 |

11. (i) What is the purpose of star markings on refrigerators and freezers?

    _____  | 2 |

    (ii) What do four stars indicate on a fridge or freezer?

    _____

    _____  | 2 |

Total Mark

**Homework Assignment 11**

| 56 |

*Teacher's comment*

_____

## Chapter 7 Preparing to Cook

Date of issue          Due date

## OL 1999, 1998, 1996

1. Describe six guidelines for kitchen safety that you should follow in cookery class.

   (i) _____

   (ii) _____

   (iii) _____

   (iv) _____

   (v) _____

   (vi) _____

   6

2. Describe the routine you should follow at the start of a cookery class.

   _____

   _____

   _____

   _____

   _____

   _____

   6

3. Name the following pieces of kitchen equipment and state one use for each item.

(i)    (ii)    (iii)

(iv)    (v)

(vi)    (vii)

| Name of kitchen equipment | Use |
|---|---|
| (i) | |
| (ii) | |
| (iii) | |
| (iv) | |
| (v) | |
| (vi) | |
| (vii) | |

14

4. Give two reasons why recipes are sometimes modified.

(i) _____

(ii) _____

4

5. Explain each of the following terms used in cookery.

| Term | Explanation |
| --- | --- |
| (i) Al dente | |
| (ii) Bake blind | |
| (iii) Baste | |
| (iv) Garnish | |
| (v) Glaze | |
| (vi) Marinade | |
| (vii) Raising agent | |
| (viii) Roux | |
| (ix) Sauté | |

18

# 13

| Chapter 8 | Cooking Food |

Date of issue                                        Due date

**HL  1999**

**OL  2005**

1.  List three reasons why food is cooked.

    (i)  _____

    (ii) _____

    (iii) _____   | 3 |

2.  What effect does cooking have on each of the following foods?

    | Food | Effect of cooking |
    | --- | --- |
    | (i)   Cheese | |
    | (ii)  Eggs | |
    | (iii) Fish | |
    | (iv)  Meat | |
    | (v)   Milk | |
    | (vi)  Vegetables | |

    | 6 |

3.  What method of heat transfer is mainly involved in each of the following cooking methods?

| Cooking method | Method of heat transfer |
|----------------|-------------------------|
| (i)   Boiling   | |
| (ii)  Frying    | |
| (iii) Grilling  | |
| (iv)  Roasting  | |
| (v)   Steaming  | |

5

4.  Suggest one advantage and one disadvantage of each of the following cooking methods.

| Cooking method | Advantage | Disadvantage |
|----------------|-----------|--------------|
| (i)   Boiling     | | |
| (ii)  Frying      | | |
| (iii) Grilling    | | |
| (iv)  Microwaving | | |
| (v)   Steaming    | | |
| (vi)  Stewing     | | |

12

5. Suggest a suitable method of cooking for each of the following.

    (i)    Pasta: _____

    (ii)   Queen cakes: _____

    (iii)  Rashers: _____

    (iv)  Whole chicken: _____

    (v)   Cooking apples: _____

    (vi)  Carrots: _____

    6

6. State how potatoes or sausages are prevented from bursting while being cooked in the microwave.

_____

    2

Total / Mark

**Homework Assignment 13**

$\overline{34}$

*Teacher's comment*

Date of issue           Due date

## Higher Level

### HL 2009, 2002

1. Give the nutritional composition of red meat.

     6

2. Outline the importance of including red meat in the diet of teenagers.

     6

3. What guidelines should be followed when buying, storing and cooking minced meat?

    (i)   Buying:

     4

    (ii)   Storing:

     4

(iii) Cooking: _____

_____

_____

_____ | 4 |

4. (i) Outline the causes of toughness in meat. _____

_____ | 4 |

(ii) List and explain three ways of tenderising red meat.

(a) _____

(b) _____

(c) _____ | 6 |

5. (i) Name one meat substitute. _____ | 2 |

(ii) What are the advantages of using meat substitutes?

_____

_____ | 4 |

6. (i) Explain the term 'offal'. _____

_____ | 2 |

| 2 |

(ii) Give one example of offal. _____

Total Mark

**Homework Assignment 14 (Higher Level)**

_____ | **44** |

*Teacher's comment*

_____

## OL 2004, 2000

1. Give two reasons why meat is important in the diet.

    (i) _____

    (ii) _____ | 4 |

2. Meat has no carbohydrate. Name two foods that you could serve with meat in order to provide carbohydrate.

    (i) _____ (ii) _____ | 2 |

3. Plan a healthy two-course lunch menu for a teenager that includes a homemade beef burger made from fresh mince.

    > *Menu*

    | 4 |

4. Give two reasons why we cook meat.

    (i) _____

    (ii) _____ | 4 |

5.  Name **four** different methods of cooking meat.

    (i) _____     (ii) _____

    (iii) _____   (iv) _____   | 4 |

6.  Name **two** main course dishes (other than the burger mentioned above) that can be made using minced meat.

    (i) _____     (ii) _____   | 2 |

7.  (i) Explain the term 'offal'. _____

    _____   | 2 |

    (ii) Give **one** example of offal. _____

    _____   | 2 |

Total Mark

**Homework Assignment 14  (Ordinary Level)**     **24**

*Teacher's comment*

Date of issue                              Due date

**HL  2000**

**OL  2003, 2001** (part of a question)

1.  For health reasons, many people are now choosing to include more poultry in their diets as opposed to red meat. Compare the nutritive value of red meat and chicken.

8

2.  Outline the rules that should be followed when buying fresh and frozen poultry.

    (i)  Fresh:

2

    (ii) Frozen:

2

3.  How should fresh poultry be stored?

    _____

    _____

    _____    | 6 |

4.  Outline how you would roast a frozen chicken weighing 2kg.

    _____

    _____

    _____

    _____    | 10 |

5.  Describe how you can reduce the dangers of food poisoning from poultry.

    _____

    _____

    _____

    _____

    _____

    _____

    _____    | 8 |

Total / Mark

**Homework Assignment 15**

| 36 |

*Teacher's comment*

_____

## Chapter 10    Fish

Date of issue                                    Due date

## Higher Level

**HL  2008, 1999** (short questions 2001, 1997)

1.  State three classifications of fish and give two examples of **each** class.

    (i)   Class 1: _____

          Examples: _____    _____

    (ii)  Class 2: _____

          Examples: _____    _____

    (iii) Class 3: _____

          Examples: _____    _____     9

2.  Give the nutritional composition of fish **and** outline its value in the diet.

    (i)   Nutritional composition: _____

          _____

          _____

          _____

          _____     10

    (ii)  Value in the diet: _____

_____

_____ | 8 |

_____

3.    What guidelines should be followed when buying **and** storing fresh fish?

    (i)  Buying: _____

_____

_____ | 8 |

    (ii)  Storing: _____

_____

_____

_____ | 8 |

4.    (i)  Suggest three methods of cooking fish.

        (a)  _____    (b)  _____

        (c)  _____ | 4 |

    (ii)  What are the effects of cooking on fish?

_____

_____

_____ | 6 |

5.    Why is lemon used to garnish fish dishes?

_____ | 4 |

6.  Suggest one other garnish suitable for fish. _____ | 2 |

7.  Describe three ways that fish are processed.

    (i)    _____    _____

    _____

    _____

    (ii)   _____

    _____

    _____

    (iii)  _____

    _____

    _____ | 6 |

Total / Mark

**Homework Assignment 16 (Higher Level)**

| 65 |

*Teacher's comment*

_____

## Ordinary Level

## OL  2007, 2002

1.  Name one fish in **each** of the following groups.

    | White fish | Oily fish | Shellfish | |
    |---|---|---|---|
    | | | | 6 |

### Composition of oily fish

| Protein | Fat | Carbohydrate | Minerals | Vitamins | Water |
|---|---|---|---|---|---|
| 17–20% | 13% | 0% | A, D, B | Iodine, iron | 65% |

2.  Using the information given above, give three reasons why oily fish should be included in the diet.

    (i) _____

    (ii) _____

    (iii) _____   6

3.  Oily fish lacks carbohydrate. Suggest two different carbohydrate foods that can be served with oily fish.

    (i) _____   (ii) _____   4

4.  Name one other nutrient that is not found in oily fish.

    _____   2

5.  Suggest three ways to encourage children to eat fish.

    (i) _____

    (ii) _____

    (iii) _____   6

6. Plan a packed lunch menu for a teenager that includes fish.

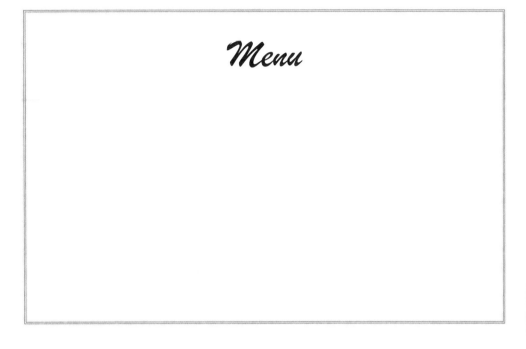

10

7. List four guidelines that should be followed when buying fresh fish.

(i) _____

(ii) _____

(iii) _____

(iv) _____

8

8. List two guidelines that should be followed when storing fresh fish.

(i) _____

(ii) _____

4

9. Name one method of processing fresh fish.

_____

2

Total Mark

**Homework Assignment 16 (Ordinary Level)**

44

*Teacher's comment*

_____

17

Date of issue                                    Due date

**HL  2007**

**OL  2009, 2005, 2001, 2000**

1.  Name two nutrients found in eggs.

    (i) _____    (ii) _____    | 4 |

2.  List three reasons why eggs are important in the diet.

    (i) _____

    _____

    _____

    (ii) _____

    _____

    _____

    (iii) _____

    _____

    _____    | 6 |

3.  Name two important nutrients not found in eggs.

    (i) _____    (ii) _____    | 2 |

4. Plan a balanced breakfast menu for a schoolgoing child to include an egg dish.

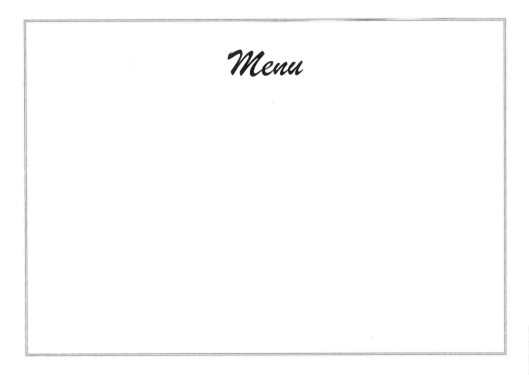

*Menu*

6

5. Name the parts of the egg labelled 1 to 6.

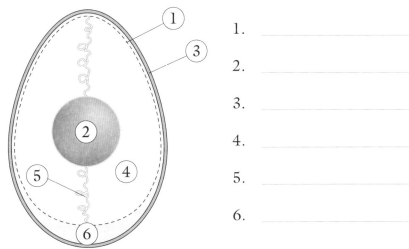

1. _____

2. _____

3. _____

4. _____

5. _____

6. _____

6

6. List **four** items of information you would expect to find on an egg box.

(i) _____

(ii) _____

(iii) _____

(iv) _____

8

7. What guidelines should be followed when buying and storing eggs?

   (i) Buying: _____

   _____ | 4 |

   (ii) Storing: _____

   _____ | 4 |

8. Explain the term 'free-range eggs'. _____

   _____ | 2 |

9. List five culinary uses of eggs and name a different dish to illustrate each use.

   | Culinary use of eggs | Dish |
   | --- | --- |

   (i)

   (ii)

   (iii)

   (iv)

   (v) | 10 |

10. Name two groups of people who should avoid eating raw eggs.

    (i) _____

    (ii) _____ | 4 |

11. What effect does cooking have on eggs?

    _____

    _____ | 4 |

Total / Mark

**Homework Assignment 17**

**60**

*Teacher's comment*

| Chapter 10 | Milk and Yoghurt |
| --- | --- |

Date of issue .                                        Due date

**HL** **2006** (long question), **1999, 1995, 1994, 1992** (short question)

**OL** **2002** (long question), **2006, 1992** (short question)

1. The following information is displayed on the label of a carton of fortified milk.

*Fortified Milk*

| NUTRITIIONAL INFORMATION Typical value per 100ml | FORTIFIED MILK | WHOLE MILK |
| --- | --- | --- |
| Energy | 205kJ/49kcal | 269kJ/64kcal |
| Protein | 3.4g | 3.3g |
| Fat | 1.5g | 3.5g |
| Carbohydrate | 5.2g | 4.9g |
| Calcium | 166mg | 118mg |
| Vitamin A | 120µg | 52µg |
| Vitamin B | 0.24mg | 0.17mg |
| Folic acid | 70µg | 6µg |
| Vitamin D | 1µg | 0.03µg |
| Vitamin E | 1.5mg | 0.09mg |

Pastuerised and Homogenised

Using the information given on the label above, evaluate the nutritive value of fortified milk.

6

2. State which type of milk would be most suitable for an energetic child and a pregnant woman. Give a reason for your choice in each case.

(i) Energetic child: ~~Super Milk~~ Whole milk

Reason: more energy & vitamins          | 3 |

(ii) Pregnant woman: ~~Sortified~~ Super milk

Reason: No fat but there is vitamins.          | 3 |

3. Name two other types of milk available in shops.

(i) Low-fat milk          (ii) Whole milk.          | 4 |

4. Explain how and why milk is pasteurised.

(i) How: heated to 72°C for 15 seconds          | 2 |

(ii) Why: kills bacteria          | 2 |

5. (i) List two dairy products, other than milk, available in supermarkets.

(a) youghurt ✓          (b) cheese ✓          | 2 |

(ii) Suggest three ways to include more dairy products in the diet.

(a) eat yoghurts ✓

(b) eat cheese ✓

(c) take glasses of milk ✓          | 6 |

6. Explain each of the following terms.

(i) Fortified: when nutrients are added ✓          | 2 |

(ii) Homogenised: spreads the cream, or fat, evenly throughout the milk. Most milk is treated in this way ✓          | 2 |

7. Suggest four ways milk may be used in food preparation.

(i) it can be added to breakfast cereals

(ii) many dishes contain milk example pancake

(iii) it is used for baking

(iv) It can be added to soups to give it a cremier taste and improve its nutritive value

4

8. List two effects of heat on milk.

(i) different flavour

(ii) bacteria are destroyed

4

9. Describe two ways milk can be processed to extend its shelf life.

(i) by heating it to 132°C

(ii) by removing some water and canning it

4

✗

10. Name and describe two different types of cream on the market today.

(i) Name: Double cream

Description: cream used in desert making

(ii) Name: Low fat cream

Description: reduced fat though still contains 30% fat

4

## Yoghurt

**11.** What is yoghurt? _____

_____

| 4 |

**12.** Name **and** describe four different types of yoghurt on the market today.

(i) Name: _____

Description: _____

(ii) Name: _____

Description: _____

(iii) Name: _____

Description: _____

(iv) Name: _____

Description: _____

| 8 |

**13.** Describe four different uses of yoghurt in cookery.

(i) _____

(ii) _____

(iii) _____

(iv) _____

| 8 |

Total Mark

**Homework Assignment 18**

| **68** |

*Teacher's comment*

| Chapter 10 | Cheese |
| --- | --- |

Date of issue                                          Due date

**H.L.**  **2001** (long question)

**O.L.**  **2006** (long question), **2003** (short question)

| Cheese | Protein | Fat | Carbohydrate | Minerals | Vitamins | Water |
| --- | --- | --- | --- | --- | --- | --- |
| **Cheddar** | 27% | 33% | 0% | 4% calcium | A, B | 34% |
| **Cottage** | 15% | 4% | 4% | 1% calcium | A, B | 77% |

1.  Using the nutritional information in the table above, state which type of cheese would be most suitable for each of the following. Give two reasons for your choice in each case.

    (i)  An adult on a low-cholesterol diet: _____ | 2 |

        Reasons: _____

        _____

        _____ | 4 |

        _____

    (ii)  An energetic teenager: _____ | 2 |

        Reasons: _____

        _____

        _____ | 4 |

2. Using **one** of the cheeses named in the table, design a balanced snack suitable for a packed lunch.

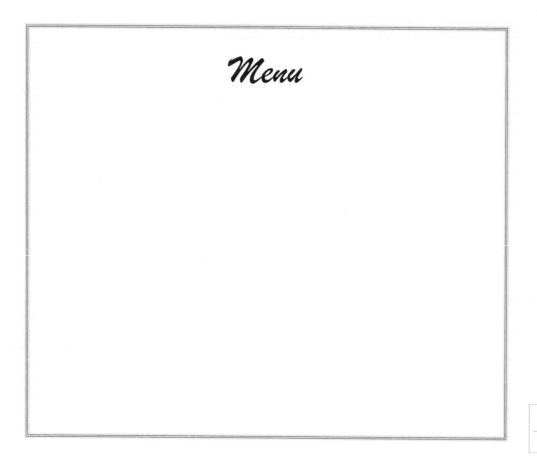

6

3. Classify cheese and give **one** example in each class.

| Type of cheese | Example |
| --- | --- |
| (i) | |
| (ii) | |
| (iii) | |

6

4. List **six** different uses of cheese in cookery.

(i) _____    (ii) _____

(iii) _____    (iv) _____

(v) _____    (vi) _____

6

5. Outline the six stages involved in the manufacture of cheese.

_____

_____

_____

_____

_____

_____ | 12 |

_____

6. Explain the term 'au gratin'.

_____ | 2 |

7. How should cheese be stored?

_____

_____ | 4 |

_____

8. Describe two effects of cooking on cheese.

(i) _____

| 4 |

(ii) _____

**Homework Assignment 19**

Total Mark

| 52 |

_Teacher's comment_

_____

Date of issue                                   Due date

**HL  2005** (long question), **2004** (short question)

**OL  2008, 2003** (long questions)

1.   Name the part of the cereal grain labelled 1 to 4.

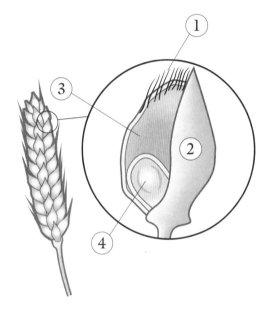

          1. _____

          2. _____

          3. _____    4

          4. _____

2.   Give two effects of cooking on cereals.

     (i) _____

                                                      4

     (ii) _____

3.   Cereals are a staple food in many countries.

     (i)   Explain why cereals are important in the diet. _____

                                                         4

          _____

(ii) Match the following products with the cereal they are made from.

bread, cooking oil, cornflakes, muesli, popcorn, porridge,
Ready Brek, rice cakes, Rice Krispies, spaghetti, Weetabix

| Maize | Oats | Wheat | Rice |
|-------|------|-------|------|
| (i) | (i) | (i) | (i) |
| (ii) | (ii) | (ii) | (ii) |
| (iii) | (iii) | (iii) | |

11

4. What is the difference between a wholegrain cereal product and a refined product?

(i) Whole-grain cereal product is: _____

_____

2

(ii) Refined cereal product is: _____

_____

2

5. Explain why some cereal products, such as breakfast cereals, may be fortified.

_____

_____

_____

2

6. Name three types of flour used in baking and suggest a different use for each.

| Type of flour | Use |
|---------------|-----|
| (i) | |
| (ii) | |
| (iii) | |

6

7. Outline how flour is processed.

_____

_____

_____ 4

8. List two types of rice available to the consumer and suggest a different dish in which each one can be used.

| Type of rice | Dish |
|---|---|
| (i) | |
| (ii) | |

4

9. Pasta has become a popular food in Ireland. The following is a label from a packet of spaghetti. Using the information provided on the label, answer **each** of the following questions.

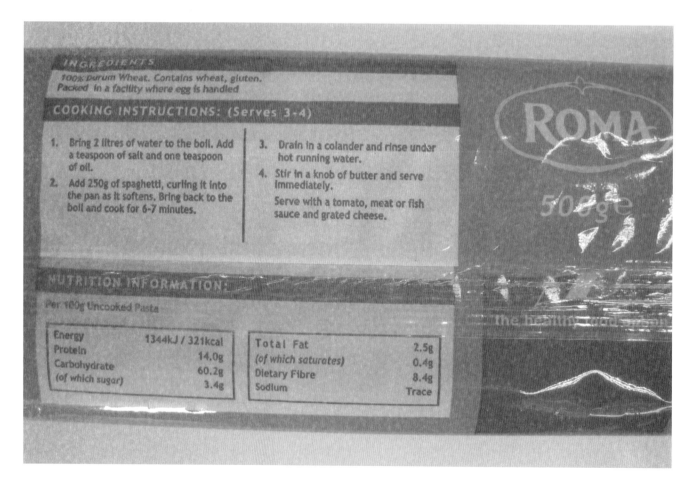

(i) What is the main ingredient in spaghetti? _____ `2`

(ii) How many kilocalories are there per 100g of spaghetti? _____ `2`

(iii) How long does it take to cook spaghetti? _____ `2`

(iv) Name one nutrient not present in spaghetti. _____ `2`

(v) Give a function of the nutrient you have named.

_____

_____ `2`

(vi) Name two pasta dishes.

(a) _____     (b) _____ `4`

10. Porridge is a healthy, wholesome breakfast cereal. The following information is displayed on a packet of porridge oatflakes. From the information given:

# Porridge Oatflakes

| NUTRITIIONAL INFORMATION | COOKING METHODS |
|---|---|
| **Per 30g serving** | Method A: Add one cup of oatflakes to three cups of milk. Boil and stir for 4–5 minutes. |
| Energy 465kJ/110kcal | **OR** |
| Protein 3.3g | Method B: Add ½ cup of oatflakes to ⅔ cup of water. Stir and place in a bowl in a microwave oven. Cook for 2–3 minutes. |
| Carbohydrate 19.8g | |
| (of which sugars) 0.3g | |
| Fat 1.5g | Note – cooking times may vary according to microwave rating. |
| (of which saturates) 0.3g | |
| Fibre 2.7g | |
| Sodium 0.003g | |

(i) Evaluate the nutritive value of the porridge oatflakes.

_____

_____

_____ `6`

(ii) Name **two** nutrients not present in the porridge oatflakes and suggest **one** way of including each nutrient at breakfast.

(a) Nutrient: _____

Way of including at breakfast: _____

_____

(b) Nutrient: _____

Way of including at breakfast: _____   | 4 |

(iii) Design a balanced breakfast menu, to include porridge, suitable for a schoolgoing teenager.

*Menu*

| 6 |

Total / Mark

**Homework Assignment 20**

| 73 |

*Teacher's comment*

| Chapter 10 | Fruit |
|---|---|

**HL  2004**

**OL  2007, 2001**

## Fruit

1.   Place **each** of the following fruits under the correct headings in the table.

1 apple                    2 plums

1 pear                     1 peach

1 orange                   100ml apple juice

6 strawberries             juice of $\frac{1}{2}$ lemon

### Classification of fruit

| Citrus | Berries | Stone | Hard |
|---|---|---|---|
| | | | |
| | | | |

8

2.  Fruit forms an important part of a balanced diet.

| Fruit | Protein | Carbohydrate | Minerals | Vitamins | Water |
|---|---|---|---|---|---|
| **Fresh** | Trace | 5–20% | Calcium, iron | A, C | 80–90% |
| **Tinned** | Trace | 20–30% | Calcium, iron | A, C reduced | 70–80% |
| **Dried** | Trace | 50–60% | Calcium, iron (increased) | A | 15–25% |

(i)  Using the information given in the table above, compare the food value of fresh fruit and tinned or dried fruit.

_____

_____

_____

_____

_____

_____

6

(ii)  Give one function of **each** mineral listed in the table.

(a)  Calcium:  _____

(b)  Iron:  _____

4

(iii)  What does 'trace' mean?  _____

_____

2

(iv)  Suggest two different uses for **each** of the types of fruit listed in the table above.

| Fresh | Tinned | Dried |
|---|---|---|
|  |  |  |

6

3. What are the advantages of including fruit in the diet? _____

_____

_____ 6

4. Give two effects of processing on fruit.

(i) _____

(ii) _____ 2

5. Describe how you would prepare each of the following fruits for a fresh fruit salad.

(i) Pear: _____

_____

(ii) Strawberries: _____

_____

(iii) Orange: _____

_____

(iv) Peach: _____

_____ 8

6. Give two advantages of buying fruit in season.

(i) _____

(ii) _____ 4

7. Suggest two ways to encourage children to eat more fruit.

(i) _____

(ii) _____ 4

Total / Mark

**Homework Assignment 21**

50

*Teacher's comment*

_____

Date of issue                                Due date

**HL  2007, 1998**

**OL  2009, 2004**

1.  Vegetables form an important part of a healthy diet.

| Vegetables | Protein | Carbohydrate | Vitamins | Minerals | Water |
|---|---|---|---|---|---|
| Root | 1–2% | 5–20% | C, A | Calcium, iron | 70–90% |
| Green | Nil | 5–10% | C, A | Calcium, iron, potassium | 90–95% |
| Pulses | 2–5% | 4–8% | C, A | Calcium, potassium | 75–90% |

Name two vegetables from each of the classes above.

(i)   Root:   _____      _____

(ii)  Green:  _____      _____

(iii) Pulse:  _____      _____

6

2.  Which class of vegetable is most useful in a vegan diet? Explain why.

(i)   Answer: _____

(ii)  Reason: _____

4

3. Give four reasons why vegetables should be included in the daily diet.

(i) _____

(ii) _____

(iii) _____

(iv) _____

`4`

4. Name one nutrient that is not present in any of the vegetables referred to in the table above and suggest one way of including it in the diet.

(i) Nutrient not present in the vegetables above: _____

(ii) Way of including it in the diet: _____

_____

`4`

5. What steps should be taken when storing, preparing and cooking vegetables in order to retain the maximum food value?

(i) Storing: _____

`4`

(ii) Preparing: _____

`4`

(iii) Cooking: _____

`4`

6. List three guidelines that should be followed when buying fresh vegetables.

(i) _____

(ii) _____

(iii) _____

`6`

7. Suggest a different vegetable for each of the following methods of cooking.

| Method | Suggested vegetable |
|---|---|
| (i)   Baking | |
| (ii)  Boiling | |
| (iii) Roasting | |
| (iv)  Stir-frying | |

☐ 4

8. Explain the term 'al dente'.

_____

_____

☐ 2

---

## FARM-FRESH STEAM VEGETABLES

A delicious variety of frozen fresh vegetables.
Gently steam to perfection ... and enjoy!

**NUTRITIONAL INFORMATION**
Typical values per serving

| | |
|---|---|
| Energy | 45 cal |
| Protein | 4.6g |
| Carbohydrate | 5.4g |
| Fat | 0.6g |
| Fibre | 3.4g |
| Sodium | Trace |
| Vitamin C | 34mg |
| Folic acid | 99µg |

**INGREDIENTS**
Carrots, green beans, baby sweetcorn, peas.

A serving of 'Farm-Fresh Steam Vegetables' provides 1 of your recommended 5 daily portions of fruit and vegetables.

For best results, steam for 5 minutes.

9. Using the information given on the product label on p. 74, evaluate the nutritive value of these 'Farm Fresh Vegetables'.

_____

_____

_____

_____

_____

_____

10

10. Design a three-course dinner menu, to include this product, suitable for a family meal.

*Menu*

6

11. Give two reasons why steaming is the recommended method of cooking for vegetables.

(i) _____

(ii) _____

4

12. How can teenagers include more vegetables in their daily diet?

4

13. Explain what is meant by organically grown vegetables.

2

14. Under EU regulations, how must vegetables be presented for sale?

6

15. How are vegetables graded?

4

16. Name **three** ways vegetables may be processed.

(i) _____     (ii) _____

(iii) _____

6

Total / Mark

**Homework Assignment 22**

84

*Teacher's comment*

| Chapter 10 | Combination Foods |
|---|---|

Date of issue                        Due date

Sometimes as part of section B, questions 1 or 2, a single-product food, e.g. meat, fish, eggs, fruit or vegetables, is not asked about, but rather a 'combination' food, i.e. a food that is composed of a number of different ingredients, such as soup (**2008, HL**; **2006 and 2000, OL**), sauces (**2003, HL**), pizza (**2002, HL**) and garlic-stuffed chicken breasts (**2000, HL**). Complete this homework assignment to practise this type of question.

### Cooking Instructions

Conventional cooking (for best results)
1. Preheat the oven to 200°C (400°F) or gas mark 6.
2. Pierce film lid and place on a baking tray.
3. Cook for 20 minutes in the top half of the oven.
4. Peel back film lid, stir sauce and replace film lid.
5. Cook for a further 20 minutes.
6. Take out of the oven and stand for 1 minute.
7. Remove film lid and stir gently before serving.

4889 121 6565

### Nutritional Information

| Typical values | Per 100g | Per serving (330g) |
|---|---|---|
| Energy | 428kj/101kcal | 1420kj/337kcal |
| Protein | 6.9g | 22.9g |
| Carbohydrates | 12.3g | 40.7g |
| (of which sugars) | (2.4g) | (8.1g) |
| Fat | 2.8g | 9.1g |
| (of which saturates) | (1.2g) | (3.9g) |
| Fibre | 0.6g | 2.0g |
| Sodium | 0.2g | 0.6g |
| Salt equivalent | 0.5g | 1.5g |

### Ingredients

Cooked pasta (28%), cooked marinated chicken (15%), chicken breast (12%), mushrooms (7%), onions and red peppers (2%), green peppers (2%), cream (2%), celery and celeriac (2%), water, rice bran oil, fructose syrup, salt, modified tapioca starch, whipping cream, lime juice powder, vegetable oil, flavourings, concentrated mushroom stock, concentrated chicken stock, chicken bouillon, garlic puree, onion powder, mustard powder, spice.

### Contains

Gluten, wheat, egg, milk, celery, celeriac, mustard.

### Dietary Information

No artificial colours.
A serving contains 1.5g of an adult's recommended daily salt intake of 6g.

1.    Using the information displayed on the label above, evaluate the nutritive value of the product.

_____

_____

_____

_____

_____

_____

10

2. Name **two** food additives listed.

   (i) _____    (ii) _____    `2`

3. What is the main ingredient in this dish? _____ `2`

4. Would this product be suitable for the following people?
Explain your answer.

   (i) A diabetic   Yes ☐   No ☐

      Reason: _____ `4`

   (ii) A coeliac   Yes ☐   No ☐

      Reason: _____ `4`

   (iii) Someone on a low-fat diet   Yes ☐   No ☐

      Reason: _____ `4`

   (iv) Vegan   Yes ☐   No ☐

      Reason: _____ `4`

5. (i) State the recommended daily salt intake for an adult.

      _____ `2`

   (ii) What effect can a high-salt diet have on the body?

      _____

      _____ `4`

6. (i) What is a thickening agent?

      _____ `2`

   (ii) Name **one** thickening agent used in this product.

      _____ `2`

7.  What precautions should be taken when buying, storing and cooking 'ready-to-cook' meals to avoid the risk of food poisoning?

    (i)   Buying: _____

    _____

    (ii)  Storing: _____

    _____

    (iii) Cooking: _____

    _____

    6

8.  Name one food-poisoning bacteria that is associated with poultry.

    _____

    2

9.  How long does it take to cook this dish?

    _____

    2

Total / Mark

**Homework Assignment 23**

*Teacher's comment*

_____

50

| Chapter 11 | Breakfasts and Packed Meals |

Date of issue ................................ Due date ................................

**HL  2005**

**OL  2008, 1994**

## Breakfast

1.  List five guidelines for planning a healthy breakfast.

    (i) Get up early and don't rush-sit down & enjoy it.

    (ii) Include food from all four food group. ✓

    (iii) It is important to include fluids. ✓

    (iv) Choose high-fibre breakfast cereals. ✓

    (v) Grill instead of fry. ✓

    | 10 |

2.  Write down three reasons why breakfast is important.

    (i) Your blood sugar is low after fasting all night. ✓

    (ii) You will be less able to concentrate at school or at work. ✓

    (iii) You're more likely to eat high-calorie mid-morning snacks. ✓

    | 6 |

3. Make out a nutritious breakfast menu for a schoolgoing teenager to include all four food groups.

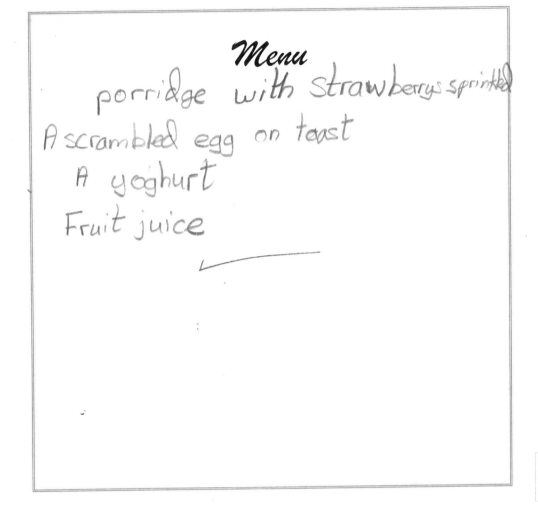

*Menu*

porridge with strawberrys sprinkled
A scrambled egg on toast
A yoghurt
Fruit juice

8

4. Give reasons for your choice of menu above.

There is a bit of the four
food groups. Porridge is very
good for you.

8

5. Name the items labelled in the diagram below of a breakfast tray.

A _Napkin_    B _toast_    C _cereal_

D _Salt & Pepper_    E _sugarcubes_    F _Butter_   $\boxed{6}$

## Packed meals

6. List **five** guidelines for planning packed meals.

(i) _Try to include all four food groups._

(ii) _Include a drink high in vitamin C._

(iii) _Try to have variety._

(iv) _Avoid empty-calorie foods._

(v) _Consider the person's likes and dislikes_   $\boxed{10}$

7. Plan a healthy packed meal for an office worker to include all four food groups.

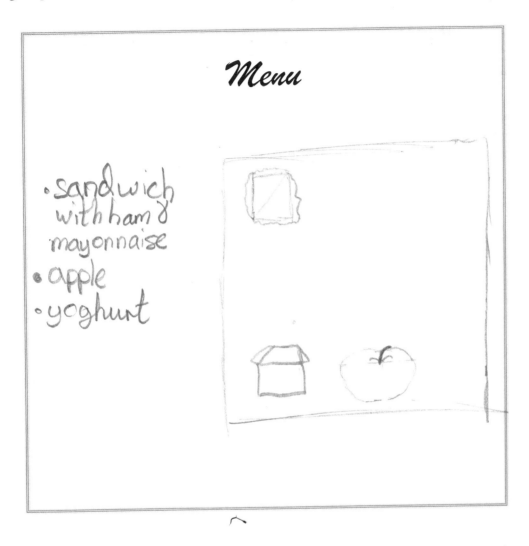

8. Give reasons for your choice of menu.

_____

_____

_____

_____

_____

9.   Imagine you were responsible for the sandwiches/rolls/wraps etc. in your school canteen. Describe four different options that you would make available to students.

(i)   Option 1: Brown Pita pocket - filled with chicken tika, cheese toasted and red onion and tika sauce.

(ii)   Option 2: Italian chesse and herb roll - filled with ham and cheese toasted and lettuce tomatoes, red onion and sweet chili mayonnaise.

(iii)   Option 3: white wrap - filled with beef tomatoes, lettuce, red onion and mayonaise

(iv)   Option 4: Two slices of brown bread - filled with tuna and sweetcorn.

8

Total / Mark

Homework Assignment 24

72

Teacher's comment

Chapter 11    Soups

Date of issue                                    Due date

**H.L.  2008**

**O.L.  2006, 2000**

Soups

1.   How are soups classified? Give two examples of soups from each class.

(i)   Class 1: Thin soup

Examples:

(a)   Clear soup

(b)   Broth

(ii)   Class 2: Thick soups

Examples:

(a)   Puréed

(b)   Thickened                                          6

2.   Describe four characteristics of a good soup.

(i)   Is made from a fresh well flavoured stock.

(ii)   Tastes of its main ingredients

(iii)   Has a good colour

(iv)   A think soup shouldn't be too thick          8
     and have starchy lumps

3. Describe three ways that soup can be thickened.

(i) Blend 25g of ~~flavoured~~ flour or cornflour with cold water. Stir in the mixture just before the end of cooking time. Bring the soup back to the boil and boil for a5 five mins

(ii) Begin by gently frying sautéing the soup ingredients. Add flour & stock

(iii) Add barley, rice or pasta.

6

4. Name three different types of convenience soup. Give one advantage and one disadvantage of each soup you have named.

(i) Convenience soup 1: Packed soup

Advantage: Cheap

Disadvantage: Not very nutrieaus

3

(ii) Convenience soup 2: Canned soup

Advantage: Conveient

Disadvantage:

3

(iii) Convenience soup 3: Carton of soup

Advantage:

Disadvantage:

3

For the rest of this homework assignment, choose either the Ordinary or Higher Level questions below.

## Higher Level

5.  The following information is displayed on the label of a carton of soup.

---

### *SOUP TO GO*
#### Chicken and Sweetcorn Soup

**NUTRITION INFORMATION**

Typical values per cup

| | |
|---|---|
| Energy | 660kj/158kcal |
| Protein | 4.1g |
| Carbohydrate | 16.0g |
| (of which sugars) | (4.1g) |
| Fat | 8.6g |
| (of which saturates) | (0.8g) |
| Fibre | 0.6h |
| Sodium | 0.7g |
| Salt equivalent | 1.9g |

Low fat

**Ingredients**

Water, sweetcorn, onions, chicken, vegetable oil, potatoes, cornflour, peppers, flavouring, skimmed milk, sugar, herbs, sodium, garlic powder, spice extract, beta carotene.

**DIETARY INFORMATION**

Suitable for a gluten-free diet. No artificial colours, flavours or preservatives.
A serving contains 1.9g of an adult's recommended daily salt intake of 6g.

---

Using the information given on the label above:

(i)  Evaluate the nutritive value of the soup.

10

(ii) Identify **three** different types of additives and outline their function in convenience foods.

(a) Additive 1: _____

Function: _____

(b) Additive 2: _____

Function: _____

(c) Additive 3: _____

Function: _____

$\boxed{9}$

(iii) What is a thickening agent? Name **one** thickening agent used in this product.

(a) A thickening agent is: _____

(b) One used in this product: _____

$\boxed{2}$

## Ordinary Level

6. The following is a label from a packet of convenience soup. Using the information given, answer **each** of the following.

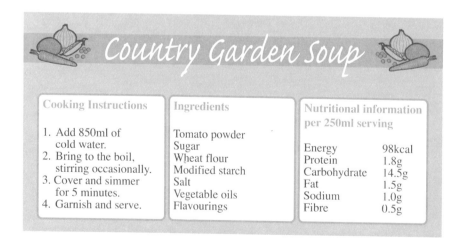

| Cooking Instructions | Ingredients | Nutritional information per 250ml serving | |
|---|---|---|---|
| 1. Add 850ml of cold water. | Tomato powder | | |
| 2. Bring to the boil, stirring occasionally. | Sugar | Energy | 98kcal |
| | Wheat flour | Protein | 1.8g |
| 3. Cover and simmer for 5 minutes. | Modified starch | Carbohydrate | 14.5g |
| | Salt | Fat | 1.5g |
| 4. Garnish and serve. | Vegetable oils | Sodium | 1.0g |
| | Flavourings | Fibre | 0.5g |

Country Garden Soup

(i) Name the main ingredient in the soup. _____ _____ · _____ | 2 |

(ii) How long should the soup be simmered for? _ _____ _____ _____ _ | 3 |

(iii) Name three nutrients found in the soup.

   (a) _ _____ · _____ _____

   (b) _____ _ · _____

   (c) _ _____ · _____ _____ | 2 |

(iv) How much fibre is provided per 250ml serving of the soup?

   _____ _____ · _____ _____ _____ _____ · _ | 2 |

(v) Suggest one way of improving the fibre content of this soup.

   _____ _____ · _ _____ · _____ | 2 |

7. The following is a recipe for fresh vegetable soup.

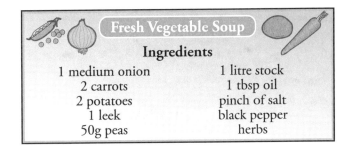

**Fresh Vegetable Soup**

**Ingredients**

| | |
|---|---|
| 1 medium onion | 1 litre stock |
| 2 carrots | 1 tbsp oil |
| 2 potatoes | pinch of salt |
| 1 leek | black pepper |
| 50g peas | herbs |

(i) Name one root vegetable and one pulse vegetable used in this recipe.

   ground

   (a) Root: Carrots ✓

   (b) Pulse: Peas ✓ | 4 |

(ii)  Plan and set out a three-course dinner menu to include vegetable soup.

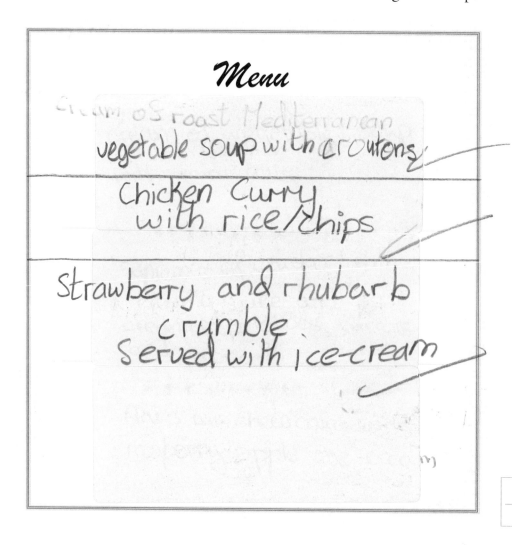

*Menu*

Cream of roast Mediterranean
vegetable soup with croutons

Chicken Curry
with rice/chips

Strawberry and rhubarb
crumble
served with ice-cream

6

(iii)  Suggest two garnishes for the soup.

(a)  croutons          (b)  swirl of cream     4

Total Mark

**Homework Assignment 25 (Higher Level)**     50

**Homework Assignment 25 (Ordinary Level)**     54

*Teacher's comment*

90

## Chapter 11    Sauces, Herbs and Spices

Date of issue                                    Due date

**HL 2003** (long question)

**OL 2007** (short question)

### Sauces

1. Complete the table below to show how sauces may be classified.
   Give one example in each class.

| Class of sauce | Example |
|---|---|
| (i) Roux based | white |
| (ii) Fruit purée | Apple |
| (iii) Egg based | Egg custard |
| (iv) Cold | Mint |
| (v) Other | chocolate |

10

2. Name the four basic roux sauce thicknesses.

   (i) binding                    (ii) coating

   (iii) Stewing                  (iv) pouring ✓

   8

3. Describe how to make a roux sauce.

   Melt fat. Add flour & seasonings, cook for 1 minute.
   Take off the heat Add milk bit by bit stir all the time
   Back on the heat Keep stirring to prevent lumping
   Bring to the boil, simmer for 5 mins, then serve

   8

4. Suggest a suitable sauce to accompany each of the following foods.

| Food | Sauce |
| --- | --- |
| (i) Apple tart | Custard |
| (ii) Bacon | Parsley |
| (iii) Beef steak | Pepper |
| (iv) Cauliflower | Cheese |
| (v) Fish | Mustard |
| (vi) Fresh pork | Apple |
| (vii) Goose | Apple |
| (viii) Lamb | Mint |
| (ix) Roast beef | Horseradish |
| (x) Turkey | Cranberry |

10

5. The following is a list of ingredients for homemade cheese sauce. Based on the ingredients listed, answer the following questions.

> **Homemade Cheese Sauce**
> 25g flour
> 50g grated cheese
> 25g margarine
> ¼ teaspoon mustard
> 500ml milk
> salt and pepper

(i) Evaluate the nutritive value of the homemade cheese sauce.

It's not packet so fresh ingredients. Convenience sauces can be higher ins ugar , salt and other additives.

8

(ii) Identify the ingredients that are combined to form a roux.

butter, flour, milk 4

(iii) Name three dishes in which cheese sauce forms part of the main ingredients.

(a) Fish            (b) Cauliflower

(c) lasenge            6

(iv) Give four reasons why sauces may be used to accompany food.

(a) Flavour            (b) less drieness

(c) Texture            (d) apperanace   8

(v) Give two advantages and two disadvantages of using convenience sauces.

(a) Advantages: Speed up preparation

(b) Disadvantages: Can be high in sugar , salt and other additives   8

## Herbs and spices

6. Give two reasons why herbs and spices are sometimes added to foods.

(i) To add flavour

(ii) To look more appetising.            4

7. Suggest one dish to which each of the herbs and spices is traditionally added.

| Herb/spice | Dish |
|---|---|
| (i) Basil | Bolognes |
| (ii) Chives | salads |
| (iii) Cinnamon | Cakes |
| (iv) Cloves | Apple tart |
| (v) Garlic | Savoury dishes |
| (vi) Mustard | ham and bacon |
| (vii) Nutmeg | Chicken |
| (viii) Sage | Stuffing |

8

Total Mark

**Homework Assignment 26**

82

*Teacher's comment*

| Chapter 12 | Food Processing and Leftovers |
| --- | --- |

Date of issue                                        Due date

**HL** 2007, 2006, 2005 (long question), 2003, 2001 (short question)

**OL** 2006, 2002, 1997

1.   Give two reasons why food is processed.

   (i) _____

   (ii) _____    | 4 |

2.   List two disadvantages of food processing for the consumer.

   (i) _____

   (ii) _____    | 4 |

3.   Name four micro-organisms that can cause food spoilage.

   (i) _____    (ii) _____

   (iii) _____    (iv) _____    | 4 |

4.   List the six conditions necessary for the growth of micro-organisms.

   (i) _____    (ii) _____

   (iii) _____    (iv) _____

   (v) _____    (vi) _____    | 6 |

5. Describe four advantages of food preservation.

(i) _____

(ii) _____

(iii) _____

(iv) _____ | 4 |

6. Explain the principle behind each of the following methods of food preservation.

| Method | Principle behind method |
|---|---|
| (i)   Canning | |
| (ii)   Drying | |
| (iii)   Freezing | |
| (iv)   Pickling | |

| 8 |

7. Outline six guidelines for successful freezing.

(i) _____

(ii) _____

(iii) _____

(iv) _____

(v) _____

(vi) _____ | 12 |

8. What is blanching? Why is it carried out?

_____

_____ | 4 |

9.  Describe each of the following methods of freezing.

    (i)  Open freezing: _____

    _____  2

    (ii)  Blast freezing: _____

    _____  2

10.  List two types of packaging suitable for use in home freezing.

    (i)  _____  (ii)  _____  2

11.  Give three pieces of advice for buying frozen foods.

    (i)  _____

    (ii)  _____

    (iii)  _____  6

12.  List six items of information that should be on food labels.

    (i)  _____  (ii)  _____

    (iii)  _____  (iv)  _____

    (v)  _____  (vi)  _____  6

13.  Give three advantages and three disadvantages of food additives.
    (i)  Advantages:

        (a)  _____

        (b)  _____

        (c)  _____  6

    (ii)  Disadvantages:

        (a)  _____

        (b)  _____

        (c)  _____  6

14. What is the function of each of the following additives in food?

| Additive | Function |
| --- | --- |
| (i)   Antioxidant | |
| (ii)  Emulsifier | |
| (iii) Flavour enhancer | |
| (iv)  Nutritional additive | |

8

15. Describe five different types of convenience foods.

(i)   _____

(ii)  _____

(iii) _____

(iv)  _____

(v)   _____

10

16. List three advantages and three disadvantages of convenience foods.

(i)  Advantages:

(a)  _____

(b)  _____

(c)  _____

6

(ii) Disadvantages:

(a)  _____

(b)  _____

(c)  _____

6

17. What are cook-chill foods?

18. Outline three guidelines for using leftovers.

(i)

(ii)

(iii)

6

19. What does the term 'rechauffé' mean?

2

20. Suggest a different dish in which would you would use **each** of the following leftover foods.

| Leftover food | Dish |
|---|---|
| (i)    Boiled potatoes | |
| (ii)   Roast turkey | |
| (iii)  Half tin of tomatoes | |

6

Total / Mark

**Homework Assignment 27**

124

*Teacher's comment*

| Chapter 13 | Home Baking |
| --- | --- |

Date of issue _____        Due date _____

**HL   2004** (long question)

**OL   2004, 2003, 2002, 2000** (short questions)

1.  List three advantages of home baking.

    (i) _____

    (ii) _____

    (iii) _____  | 6 |

2.  What guidelines should be followed when home baking?

    _____

    _____

    _____

    _____

    _____

    _____  | 12 |

3.  List three raising agents and explain how one of them works.

    (i)  Three raising agents:

         (a) _____     (b) _____     (c) _____

    (ii)  How one works:

    _____

    _____  | 5 |

4. Explain the function of gluten in bread making.

_____

_____ 4

5. Sketch the symbol found
   on gluten-free products.

4

6. List the five different methods of making bread and cakes and give two
   examples for each one.

| Method | Examples |
| --- | --- |
| (i) | |
| (ii) | |
| (iii) | |
| (iv) | |
| (v) | |

15

7. How would you prepare the tin before baking each of the following?

   (i) Bread: _____

   (ii) Fruit cakes: _____

   (iii) Small cakes: _____

   (iv) Fatless sponge: _____

   (v) Pastry: _____ 10

8. List four different types of pastry and suggest a different dish for each one.

| Pastry | Suggested dish |
|---|---|
| (i) | |
| (ii) | |
| (iii) | |
| (iv) | |

8

9. Describe six guidelines for successful pastry making.

(i) _____

(ii) _____

(iii) _____

(iv) _____

(v) _____

(vi) _____

12

10. Give two advantages and two disadvantages of commercial cake mixes.

(i) Advantages:

(a) _____

(b) _____

4

(ii) Disadvantages:

(a) _____

4

(b) _____

Total / Mark

**Homework Assignment 28**

84

*Teacher's comment*

# Unit 2

# Consumer Studies

Date of issue                                    Due date

**HL 2007, 2004, 2003, 1998**

**OL 2004**

Some part of this chapter comes up almost every year at both Higher and Ordinary Level.

1.  What is a consumer? _Buyer_ _____

    _____  | 2 |

2.  Explain the difference between needs and wants. Give examples in your answer.

    _____

    _____  | 4 |

3.  Name two factors that influence a consumer's needs and wants.

    (i) _____

    (ii) _____  | 4 |

4.  What are impulse buying and buyer's remorse?

    (i)  Impulse buying is: buying at the spur of the moment

    (ii) Buyer's remorse is: buying something that you will regret  | 4 |

5. Imagine you are buying a new mobile phone. List six factors that you would consider before purchasing.

(i) Money

(ii) Value

(iii) Brand name

(iv) Design

(v) Durability

(vi) after-sales services

12

6. List four sources of consumer information.

(i) Word of mouth (ii) Adverts

(iii) Newpapers (iv) 6 Internet

4

7. Suggest four modern-day changes that have influenced shopping trends.

(i) increase of shopping centres

(ii) Internet shopping

(iii) late opening / Sunday shopping

(iv) Self-services shopping

8

8. Give two advantages and two disadvantages of self-service shopping.

(i) Advantages:

(a)

(b)

4

(ii) Disadvantages:

(a)

(b)

4

9. Describe **each** of the following types of shopping outlet.

(i) Department store: Very large shops divided into different departments

(ii) Specialist shop: Usually sell only one type of product

(iii) Independent shop: Traditionally family-run shops usually open till late and on Sundays. Limited choice of goods

(iv) Multiple chain store: These are large large self-service shops. Branches are all owned by same company

8

10. This is an example of a bar code that can be found on many products. Why are barcodes used?

```
41689 30049
```

to allow customer to see what they bought on their receipt

4

11. What are customer loyalty cards? What advantage do they have for the consumer and the retailer?

(i) What they are: earn points when you shop

3

(ii) Advantages

(a) Consumer: you build up points for gifts

(b) Retailer: have name, address and record of your shopping

4

**12.** List four techniques used by supermarkets to encourage consumers to buy more goods.

(i) A large trolley is provided for you to fill

(ii) Mirrors lighting and colour give fruit and veg a wholesome, fresh look

(iii) Luxury items are placed at eye level

(iv) Sweets and toiletries are placed at checkouts for impulse buys

8

**13.** (i) Name three methods of payment that can be used when shopping.

(a) Cash

(b) Cheque and Cheque Card

(c) Credit Card

6

(ii) Give one advantage and one disadvantage of each method listed.

| Method of payment | Advantage | Disadvantage |
| --- | --- | --- |
| Cash | less likely to overspend and get into debt | if it's lost or stolen there is nothing you can do about it |
| Credit Card | no interest is charged | easy to overspend |
| Debit card | you can get cash back | easy to overspend |

9

**14.** Explain the benefit to the consumer of **each** of the following.

(i) Unit pricing: Goods are priced per unit

(ii) Bulk buying: buying a product in large quantities

(iii) Own brands: plaining packeted products, often good quality and are much cheaper than branded products

(iv) Keeping a receipt: knows how much you spent or you could return an item and have proof of purchase

8

15. What is meant by a loss leader?

These are goods sold off cheaply by the retailer.
It is hoped that these will lead you into the shop, where
you'll buy more

4

16. List **four** items of information that you would expect to find on a receipt.

(i) opening hours/days

(ii) phone number of shop

(iii) product & price

(iv) Name of shop

4

**Chapter 16**  Advertising

Date of issue                                      Due date

**HL  2005, 2002, 2000, 1994**

**OL  2008, 2007, 2003, 2001**

1.   List four sources/methods of advertising.

   (i)   _____        (ii)  _____

   (iii)  _____        (iv)  _____        4

2.   (i)   Describe an advertisement on television that you would consider to
         be effective.

         _____

         _____

   (ii)  Why do you think this advertisement is effective?

         _____

         _____        4

3.   List four different advertising techniques used by advertisers to encourage
      you to buy their products.

   (i)   _____        (ii)  _____

   (iii)  _____        (iv)  _____        4

4.  Give three advantages and three disadvantages of advertising.

    (i)   Advantages:

          (a) _____

          (b) _____

          (c) _____

    (ii)  Disadvantages:

          (a) _____

          (b) _____

          (c) _____      12

5.  What is the role of the Advertising Standards Authority in Ireland?

    _____

    _____      4

6.  What is the purpose of market research?

    _____

    _____      4

Total Mark

**Homework Assignment 30**

**32**

*Teacher's comment*

| Chapter 17 | Consumer Protection and Making a Complaint |
|---|---|

Date of issue                                   Due date

There is usually something from this chapter on the exam every year at both Higher and Ordinary Level.

1.    Outline four consumer rights and four consumer responsibilities.

    (i)   Rights:

        (a) _____

        (b) _____

        (c) _____

        (d) _____     8

    (ii)  Responsibilities:

        (a) _____

        (b) _____

        (c) _____

        (d) _____     8

2.  Name **two** consumer laws and explain how **each** protects the consumer.

    (i)  Law 1: _____

    How it protects the consumer:

    _____

    _____

    _____

    _____

    _____ ⎡ ⎤
                                                          ⎣6⎦

    (ii) Law 2: _____

    How it protects the consumer:

    _____

    _____

    _____

    _____

    _____ ⎡ ⎤
                                                          ⎣6⎦

3.  What is meant by a monopoly? Is a monopoly good for the consumer?
    Explain why or why not.

    _____

    _____

    _____ ⎡ ⎤
                                                          ⎣6⎦

4. (i) A mobile phone, still under guarantee, becomes faulty. List three forms of redress available to the consumer in this situation.

(a) _____

(b) _____

(c) _____   6

(ii) Write the consumer's letter of complaint to the shop where the mobile phone was bought.

10

(iii) What is a guarantee? _____

2

(iv) When is a consumer not covered by the terms of a guarantee?

2

5. Give one function of each of the following agencies.

| Agency | Function |
|---|---|
| (i) The Ombudsman | |
| (ii) National Consumer Agency | |

6. Name one non-statutory agency that provides consumer information and advice.

_____

2

7. (i) What is the function of the small claims court?

_____

_____

2

(ii) Give two advantages of the small claims procedure.

(a) _____

(b) _____

4

Total Mark

**Homework Assignment 31**

62

_Teacher's comment_

_____

Date of issue                                    Due date

Students are required to identify various quality symbols most years in section A (at both Higher and Ordinary Level). This chapter features in section B less frequently, for example **HL 2001** (packaging) and **OL 2006** (packaging).

1.  List three characteristics of a quality service.

    (i)  ~~Staff.~~ _wheelchair access_ ✓

    (ii) ~~Politeness~~ _clean toilets._ ✓

    (iii) ~~Staff.~~ _blue badge_ ✓                    | 6 |

2.  What is meant by the term 'quality control'?

    _looking after your clothes_ ✓

    | 2 |

3.  List four items of information you would expect to find on a product label attached to a bottle of household cleaning fluid.

    (i)  _clear_                   (ii) _gloves_

    (iii) ~~~~ _protect_           (iv) _do not use in_        | 4 |

4. Name each of the following symbols and write down what information each conveys to the consumer.

| Symbol | Name of symbol and information the symbol conveys to consumer |
|--------|--------------------------------------------------------------|
| (i) | |
| (ii) | |
| (iii) | |
| (iv) | |
| (v) | |
| (vi) | |
| (vii) | |
| (viii) | |
| (ix) | |

20

5. What is the function of a care label on clothing?

_____

_____  2

6. The cost of packaging adds to the consumer's shopping bill. Give four reasons why packaging of goods is necessary.

(i) _____

(ii) _____

(iii) _____

(iv) _____  8

7. What are the characteristics of good packaging?

(i) _____   (ii) _____

(iii) _____   (iv) _____  4

8. List three types of packaging and suggest a different use for **each**.

(i) Type 1: _____   Use: _____  2

(ii) Type 2: _____   Use: _____  2

(iii) Type 3: _____   Use: _____  2

9. List four disadvantages of over-packaging.

(i) _____

(ii) _____

(iii) _____

(iv) _____  8

Total / Mark

**Homework Assignment 32**

60

*Teacher's comment*

_____

Date of issue                                    Due date

There are always one or two questions from this chapter in section A at both Higher and Ordinary Levels. Money management is also a frequent topic in section B (**HL 2008, 2003, 1998, 1995** and **OL 2008, 2002, 1997**).

1.  What is a budget?

    _____    2

2.  State four advantages of budgeting.

    (i)   _____

    (ii)  _____

    (iii) _____

    (iv)  _____    8

3.  Explain the five steps involved in the money management process.

    (i)   _____

    (ii)  _____

    (iii) _____

    (iv)  _____

    (v)   _____    10

4.  Explain the difference between gross and net income.

    _____

    _____    4

5.  What do these letters stand for and what do they mean?

    (i)  PAYE: _____

    _____  [4]

    (ii)  PRSI: _____

    _____  [4]

6.  In relation to income, explain the difference between statutory deductions and voluntary deductions. Give one example of **each** type of deduction.

    (i)  Difference: _____

    (ii)  Examples:

        (a)  Statutory: _____

        (b)  Voluntary: _____  [6]

7.  What are tax credits? _____

    _____  [4]

8.  List four major expenses that should be included in a household budget.

    (i)  _____     (ii)  _____

    (iii)  _____     (iv)  _____  [4]

9.  List three advantages of saving for an item instead of buying on credit.

    (i)  _____

    (ii)  _____

    (iii)  _____  [6]

10.  Name two places where a consumer can save money.

    (i)  _____     (ii)  _____  [4]

11. List two things that the consumer should take into account before deciding on where to save their money.

    (i) _____

    (ii) _____  | 4 |

12. List two advantages of having a bank account.

    (i) _____

    (ii) _____  | 4 |

13. What is the difference between a deposit and a current account?

    _____

    _____  | 4 |

14. List one advantage and one disadvantage of buying on credit.

    (i) Advantage: _____

    (ii) Disadvantage: _____  | 4 |

15. List four different sources of credit.

    (i) _____  (ii) _____

    (iii) _____  (iv) _____  | 4 |

16. List three advantages of a home filing system.

    (i) _____

    (ii) _____

    (iii) _____  | 6 |

Total / Mark

**Homework Assignment 33**

| 82 |

*Teacher's comment*

_____

# Unit 3

# Social Studies

Chapter 20    The Family

Date of issue                                    Due date

**HL** **2005, 1995** (long question)**, 2004, 2001, 2000** (short question)
**OL** **2007, 2000** (long question)**, 2005, 2004, 2003, 2002, 2000,
    1994** (short question)

1.  Name and describe two different types of family structure.

    (i)   Structure 1: _____

    _____

    _____

    (ii)  Structure 2: _____

    _____

    _____  6

2.  Outline three changes to family life in recent years.

    (i)   _____

    (i)   _____

    (iii) _____  6

3.  State the functions of the family.

    _____

    _____

    _____  6

4. Give three physical and three emotional needs provided by the family.

| Physical | Emotional |
|---|---|
| (i) | (i) |
| (ii) | (ii) |
| (iii) | (iii) |

6

5. Outline the rights of children within the family.

4

6. What responsibilities do adolescents have within the family?

6

7. What is meant by 'role confusion'? Why might this cause conflict within the family?

6

8.  What is meant by **each** of the the following terms?

    (i) Blended family: _____

    _____

    (ii) Co-habiting couple: _____

    _____

    (iii) Dysfunctional family: _____

    _____

    (iv) Gender role: _____

    _____

    (v) Stereotype: _____

    _____ | 10 |

9.  Describe the role of the family in encouraging gender equality.

    _____

    _____

    _____

    _____

    _____ | 6 |

Total Mark

**Homework Assignment 34**

| 56 |

*Teacher's comment*

_____

## Homework Assignment 35

| Chapter 21 | Growth and Development |

Date of issue                    Due date

**HL** 2007, 2002 (long question), almost every year as a short question

**OL** 2009 (long question) 2007, 2004, 2001, 1999, 1996, 1994 (short question)

1. List four stages of human development.

   (i) _____    (ii) _____

   (iii) _____   (iv) _____    | 4 |

2. Explain the following in relation to human development.

   (i) Physical development: _____

   _____

   (ii) Mental development: _____

   _____

   (iii) Language development: _____

   _____

   (iv) Emotional development: _____

   _____

   (v) Social and moral development: _____

   _____    | 10 |

3.  List three physical changes that occur in boys and girls during puberty.

| Boys | Girls |
| --- | --- |
| (i) | (i) |
| (ii) | (ii) |
| (iii) | (iii) |

6

4.  (i)  Describe the three ways that David Elkind believes adolescents think differently to adults.

(a) _____

_____

(b) _____

_____

(c) _____

_____

6

(ii)  Do you agree with his theory? Explain your answer.

_____

_____

_____

_____

_____

_____

6

5.  (i)  What is a peer group?

_____

_____  2

(ii)  What is meant by the term 'peer pressure'?

_____

_____  2

6.  Describe two positive ways and two negative ways that adolescents may be influenced by their peers.

(i)  Positive:

(a)  _____

(b)  _____

(ii)  Negative:

(a)  _____

(b)  _____  4

7.  Explain the term 'norms'.

_____

_____  2

Total / Mark

**Homework Assignment 35**

**42**

*Teacher's comment*

_____

Date of issue                                        Due date

This section on reproduction comes up almost every year as a short question at both Higher and Ordinary Level. To date (**2009**), it has only come up as a long question once at both levels. (**2007, HL and 2003, OL**). Generally in this section you are asked to label a diagram of either the male or female reproductive system or asked to define certain terms, e.g. menopause, fertilisation.

1.   Label the diagram below of the female reproductive system.

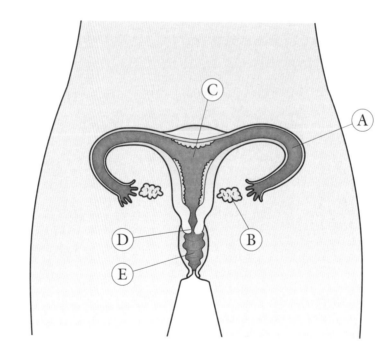

A  _____          B  _____

C  _____          D  _____

E  _____

8

2. Briefly describe the menstrual cycle.

_____

_____

_____

_____

_____

_____

_____

_____

10

3. Label the diagram below of the male reproductive system.

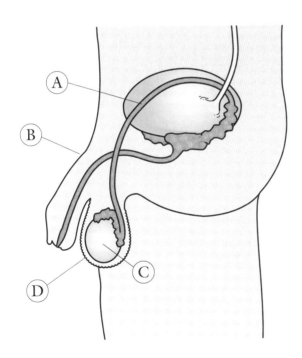

A _____    B _____

C _____    D _____

8

129

4. Outline the function of each of the following.

(i)    Placenta: _____

_____

(ii)   Fallopian tube: _____

_____

(iii)  Scrotum: _____

_____

(iv)   Uterus: _____

_____

(v)    Progesterone: _____

_____

(vi)   Testosterone: _____

_____

(vii)  Testes: _____

_____

(viii) Umbilical cord: _____

_____

(ix)   Oestrogen: _____

_____

(x)    Testes: _____

_____

(xi)   Sperm duct: _____

_____

22

5. What does each of the following terms mean?

   (i)   Ovulation: _____ _____

   _____

   (ii)  Implantation: _____

   _____

   (iii) Fertilisation: _____

   _____

   (iv)  Episiotomy: _____

   _____ | 8 |

6. Suggest four guidelines that women should follow to promote a healthy pregnancy.

   (i)   _____

   (ii)  _____

   (iii) _____

   (iv)  _____ | 8 |

7. Outline two dangers associated with casual sex.

   (i)   _____

   (ii)  _____ | 4 |

Total Mark

**Homework Assignment 36**

| 68 |

*Teacher's comment*

_____

Date of issue                              Due date

**HL  2006, 2001** (long question), **2009, 2008, 2005, 2000** (short questions)

**OL  2008, 2004, 1999** (long question), **2005, 2003, 2002, 1997, 1996** (short questions)

1. What are a baby's first set of teeth called? How many teeth are in this first set?

   20 milk teeth

   | 4 |

2. This diagram shows an adult's permanent teeth. Name the types of permanent teeth labelled A to D and state one function of each type.

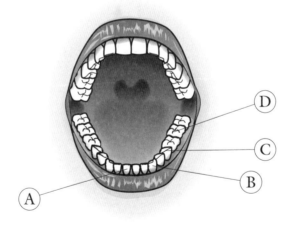

| Name of tooth | Function |
|---|---|
| A  incisors | biting |
| B  canine | tearing |
| C  pre-molars | grinding |
| D  molars | grinding |

| 8 |

3. Name the parts of the tooth labelled A to D.

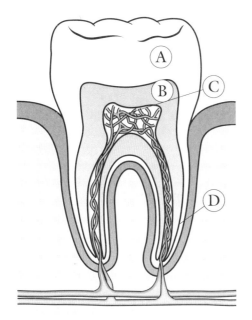

A _enamel_

B _dentine_

C _pulp cavity_

D _cementum_

4

4. Choose the correct word from the following list to complete **each** of the sentences.

crown     root     cementum     enamel     pulp cavity

(i) Most of the tooth is protected by a hard substance called

_enamel._

(ii) The _cementum_ holds the tooth in place in the jaw.

(iii) The space at the centre of the tooth is called the

_pulp cavity_

(iv) The visible part of the tooth is called the _crown_ .

(v) The _root_ of the tooth is embedded in the gum.

5

5. Why is it important to have healthy teeth?

_look unattractive, have bad breath suffer from gum and stomach infections_

5

6. Suggest four guidelines to ensure healthy teeth and gums.

(i) Remember brush twice a day,

(ii) Brush outer, inner, chewing and between teeth

(iii) Use mouthwash

(iv) Replace your brush regularly

8

7. Briefly explain how diet affects the teeth. Fizzy drinks rot your teeth

4

8. What is plaque? How does it affect the teeth?

4

9. What mineral is added to water supplies to help strengthen teeth?

2

10. What is the advantage of using **each** of the following oral hygiene products?

(i) Floride toothpaste: _____

(ii) Dental floss: _____

(iii) Antiseptic mouthwash: _____

(iv) Disclosing tablet: _____

8

11. Name two problems that are the result of poor dental hygiene.

(i) _____ (ii) _____

4

Total Mark

**Homework Assignment 37**

56

Teacher's comment

Date of issue                                    Due date

**HL**  **2008**, **1999** (long question), **2003**, **2001** (short question)

**OL**  **2005**, **2001**, **1996** (long question), **2009**, **2008**, **2006**, **2004**, **2000**, **1998**, **1997** (short question)

1.   Name two excretory organs.

(i) _____     (ii) _____     4

2.   Name the parts of the skin labelled A to D.

A _____

B _____

C _____

D _____

4

3.   Give four functions of the skin.

(i) _____

(ii) _____

(iii) _____

(iv) _____     8

4. Match the following parts of the skin with the correct function listed in the table below.

nerves, sweat glands, oil glands, fat cells, blood vessels

| Function | Part of skin |
|---|---|
| Energy reserve | |
| Feel sensations, e.g. heat | |
| Lubricate and keep the skin soft | |
| Removal of waste products | |
| Nourish skin and regulate body temperature | |

10

5. Suggest four guidelines that should be followed for healthy skin.

(i) _____

(ii) _____

(iii) _____

(iv) _____

8

6. What causes body odour?

_____

_____

4

7. List five guidelines that should be followed to ensure good personal hygiene.

(i) _____

(ii) _____

(iii) _____

(iv) _____

(v) _____

10

8.  How can overexposure to the sun damage skin?

_____

_____  [ 4 ]

9.  Give two guidelines that should be followed when sunbathing.

    (i)  _____

    (ii) _____  [ 4 ]

10. List three ways to help prevent the spread of acne.

    (i)   _____

    (ii)  _____

    (iii) _____  [ 6 ]

11. What special guidelines should be followed by teenagers when caring for their feet and toenails?

    _____

    _____

    _____

    _____  [ 8 ]

12. List four guidelines for caring for the hair.

    (i)   _____

    (ii)  _____

    (iii) _____

    (iv)  _____  [ 8 ]

13. How should long hair be cared for?

_____

_____

_____

_____

8

Total Mark

**Homework Assignment 38**

86

_Teacher's comment_

_____

Chapter 23     The Human Body – Respiratory System

Date of issue                              Due date

**The respiratory system has not come up to date (2009) at either level as a long question.**
**HL  2007, 2005, 2002, 1997** (short question)
**OL  2006, 1997, 1994** (short question)

1.   Name the parts of the respiratory system labelled A to D.

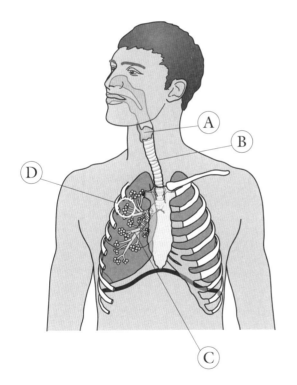

A _____

B _____

C _____

D _____

4

2.   Give two functions of the lungs.

(i) _____

(ii) _____

4

3. Complete the table below by matching each of the following parts of the respiratory system with its function: (i) nose (ii) larynx (iii) lungs (iv) epiglottis.

| Function | Part |
|---|---|
| Stops food going down the wrong way | |
| Produces sound when we speak | |
| Filters and warms air before it enters the body | |
| Exchanges carbon dioxide with oxygen | |

8

4. State two differences between the fresh air we breathe in and the stale air we breathe out by completing the sentences below.

(i) Fresh air contains _____ oxygen than stale air.

(ii) Stale air contains _____ carbon dioxide ($CO_2$) than fresh air.

4

**Homework Assignment 39**

20

*Teacher's comment*

Chapter 23     The Human Body – The Circulatory System

Date of issue                Due date

**HL**   **2009, 2004, 2000** (long question), **2007, 2006, 2004, 2003, 2002, 1999, 1995** (short question)

**OL**   **This topic is not asked at Ordinary Level except in relation to guidelines for the prevention of heart disease.**

1. What is the function of the circulatory system?

     4

2. Describe the position of the heart.

     4

3. Name the parts of the heart labelled 1 to 6.

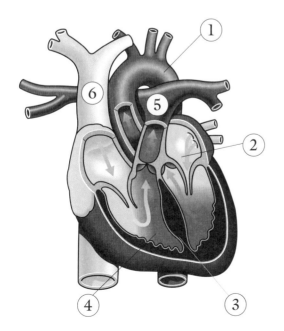

1. _____

2. _____

3. _____

4. _____

5. _____

6. _____

4.  Explain the differences between veins and arteries.

    _____

    _____

    _____    6

5.  What is the function of haemoglobin?

    _____    2

6.  Name four different blood constituents and state the function of each.

    **Blood constituent**                    **Function**

    (i)

    (ii)

    (iii)

    (iv)                                                  8

7.  What is a pulse? Describe how the pulse is taken.

    _____

    _____

    _____    4

8.  What is coronary heart disease?

    _____

    _____    4

9. Make a list of **four** guidelines for the prevention of coronary heart disease.

(i) _____

_____

(ii) _____

_____

(iii) _____

_____

(iv) _____

| 8 |

_____

Total Mark

**Homework Assignment 40**

| 46 |

*Teacher's comment*

_____

Date of issue                                    Due date

At the time of writing (**2009**), health education has come up only rarely in recent years at **Higher Level** as a long question (**2001**, **1998** and **1996**). However, this section comes up virtually every year as a short question. At **Ordinary Level**, this section has come up as a long question three times (**2006**, **2002** and **1997**). Each time the topic was smoking and to define addiction. The section comes up every year in the short questions.

1.  Define health.

    |   |
    |---|
    | 4 |

2.  Suggest four guidelines for a healthy lifestyle.

    (i)

    (ii)

    (iii)

    (iv)

    |   |
    |---|
    | 8 |

3.  List two benefits of taking regular exercise.

    (i)

    (ii)

    |   |
    |---|
    | 4 |

4.  Give two reasons why it is important to get enough sleep.

    (i)

    (ii)

    |   |
    |---|
    | 4 |

5. What is aerobic exercise?

| 2 |

6. Give two examples of aerobic exercise that would benefit teenagers.

(i) _____ (ii) _____

| 4 |

7. What is mental health?

_____

_____

| 4 |

8. Suggest four guidelines for good mental health.

(i) _____

(ii) _____

(iii) _____

(iv) _____

| 4 |

9. Tick the correct answer. Having high self-esteem means:

(i) Treating males and females equally. ☐

(ii) Feeling confident and believing in yourself. ☑

(iii) Being able to tell right from wrong. ☐

| 2 |

10. List three harmful effects of stress on the individual.

(i) _____

(ii) _____

(iii) _____

| 6 |

11. Make two suggestions to help someone suffering from stress.

(i) _____

(ii) _____

| 4 |

12. Choose the correct word from the following list to complete **each** of the sentences.

> inhale    bronchitis    exhale    nicotine    carbon dioxide

(i)   To ___ _____ means to breathe in oxygen.

(ii)   A harmful substance found in cigarettes is _____.

(iii)   Stale air contains more _____ than fresh air.

(iv)   An example of a respiratory disease is _____.

8

13. Suggest three reasons why teenagers smoke.

(i)   _____

(ii)   _____

(iii)   _____

6

14. Give two disadvantages of smoking.

(i)   _____

(ii)   _____

4

15. What is passive smoking?

_____

_____

2

16. (i)   What information does this symbol convey to the consumer?

_____

_____

_____

No smoking
It is against the law
to smoke in these
premises

2

(ii)   Name two places where you would expect to find this symbol displayed.

(a) _____        (b) _____

2

17. Describe two ways the government tries to discourage people from smoking.

(i) _____

(ii) _____  | 4 |

18. What is meant by addiction?

_____

_____  | 4 |

19. Suggest three reasons why people abuse substances.

(i) _____

(ii) _____

(iii) _____  | 6 |

20. What steps have been taken to reduce alcohol consumption in Ireland?

(i) _____

(ii) _____  | 4 |

21. List three effects of long-term alcohol abuse on each of the following.

(i) Individual: _____

_____

_____

(ii) Family: _____

_____

_____

(iii) Society: _____

_____  | 18 |

22. Explain what is meant by controlled drugs.

_____

_____ | 2 |

23. List three effects of drug use on each of the following.

   (i)  Individual: _____

_____

   (ii)  Family: _____

_____

   (iii) Society: _____ | 18 |

_____

24. What is meant by health promotion?

_____

_____ | 4 |

Total / Mark

**Homework Assignment 41**

| 130 |

*Teacher's comment*

_____

# Unit 4

# Resource Management and Home Studies

Date of issue

Due date

To date (**2009**) there has not been a question on this section at either Higher or Ordinary Level.

1.  Define home management. _____

    _____ | 2 |

2.  List six important tasks involved in running the home.

    (i) _____  (ii) _____

    (iii) _____  (iv) _____

    (v) _____  (vi) _____ | 6 |

3.  Name four resources available to the home manager.

    (i) _____  (ii) _____

    (iii) _____  (iv) _____ | 4 |

4.  List the five steps involved in a good home management system.

    (i) _____  (ii) _____

    (iii) _____  (iv) _____

    (v) _____ | 5 |

**Total Mark**

**Homework Assignment 42**

| 17 |

*Teacher's comment*

Date of issue                               Due date

This section comes up almost every year at **Higher Level** in the short questions. It does not come up as often in the short questions at **Ordinary Level**, but when it does, students are normally asked to identify one warm and one cool colour. This topic comes up fairly regularly at both levels as a long question – usually you are asked to design a room (**HL 2008, 2004, 1998**; **OL 2006, 2002, 1996**).

1.  List the factors that should be considered when choosing a family home.

_____

_____

_____    | 8 |

_____

2.  Explain each of the following room planning terms.

(i)  Proportion: _____

_____

(ii)  Balance: _____

_____

(iii)  Rhythm: _____

_____

(iv)  Emphasis: _____    | 8 |

_____

3.  Why is good lighting important in the home?

    _____

    _____ `4`

4.  What is meant by the term 'ergonomics'?

    _____

    _____ `2`

5.  What is the work triangle? Explain its importance in kitchen design.

    _____

    _____

    _____ `4`

6.  List **four** guidelines that should be followed when designing a kitchen.

    (i)   _____

    (ii)  _____

    (iii) _____

    (iv)  _____ `8`

7.  Name **one** primary and **one** secondary colour.

    (i)  Primary: _____

    (ii) Secondary: _____ `2`

8.  Name **one** cool and **one** warm colour.

    (i)  Cool: _____

    (ii) Warm: _____ `2`

9.  Explain the term 'upholstery'.

    _____

    _____ `4`

10. What are soft furnishings?

_____

_____  | 4 |

11. (i) List the factors that should be considered when planning a teenager's study-bedroom.

_____

_____

_____  | 8 |

_____

(ii) Draw the room plan of the study-bedroom, indicating the position of the door, the window, the heat source and suitable furniture.

| 12 |

(iii) Suggest **two** different types of lighting that could be used in the study-bedroom and give a reason for **each** one.

| Type of lighting | Reason for choice |
|---|---|
| (i) | |
| (ii) | |

| |
|---|
| 4 |

(iv) Suggest a colour scheme, a floor covering and soft furnishings for the room and give reasons for your suggestions in each case.

(a) Colour scheme: _____

_____

Reasons for choice of colour scheme: _____

_____

(b) Floor covering: _____

_____

Reasons for choice of floor covering: _____

_____

(c) Soft furnishings: _____

_____

Reasons for choice of soft furnishings: _____

| |
|---|
| 12 |

_____

(v) Suggest some ways in which the room could be made to reflect your personality or your hobby.

_____

_____

_____   _____

4

Total

Mark

**Homework Assignment 43**

86

_Teacher's comment_

_____

Date of issue                              Due date

This section comes up almost every year at both levels in the short questions.
It also appears occasionally as a long question at both levels

**HL   2008, 2006**

**OL   2007, 1998**

1. Name two wires in an electrical plug and state the colour(s) of **each** wire named.

| Name of wire | Colour(s) |
|---|---|
| (i) | |
| (ii) | |

4

2. What is the purpose of a fuse in an electrical plug?

2

3. List four precautions that should be taken when using electricity in the home.

(i) _____

(ii) _____

(iii) _____

(iv) _____

8

4. What two types of gas are available to households in Ireland?

(i) _____  (ii) _____

2

5. What actions should be taken in the event of a suspected gas leak in the home?

_____

_____

_____

_____   **8**

6. Why is chlorine added to domestic water supplies?

_____   **2**

7. Describe two ways a domestic water supply can be heated.

(i) _____

(ii) _____   **4**

8. Give two reasons why kitchen sinks are usually placed under a window.

(i) _____

(ii) _____   **4**

9. Describe how you would unblock a sink.

_____

_____

_____   **4**

10. What should be done in the event of burst pipes?

_____

_____   **4**

11. Name and describe two different types of artificial lighting in the home.

(i) _____

(ii) _____   **4**

12. (i) What is meant by compact fluorescent lights (CFLs)?

    _____ | 2 |

    (ii) Why are CFL bulbs used in the home?

    _____ | 2 |

13. Name the three different methods of heat transfer. Give one example of a type of home heating for each method.

| Method of heat transfer | Type of home heating |
| --- | --- |
| (i) | |
| (ii) | |
| (iii) | |

| 6 |

14. List two advantages of central heating.

    (i) _____

    (ii) _____ | 4 |

15. (i) Name four fuels used for home heating.

    (a) _____     (b) _____

    (c) _____     (d) _____ | 4 |

    (ii) Give two advantages and two disadvantage of one fuel you have named.

    (a) Fuel: _____

    (b) Advantages: _____

    _____

    (c) Disadvantages: _____

    _____ | 4 |

16. List two ways of saving energy when using a central heating system.

(i) _____

(ii) _____

| 4 |

17. What is the function of a thermostat?

_____

| 2 |

18. (i) What is the purpose of insulation?

_____

| 2 |

(ii) Name a different type of insulation suitable for **each** of the following areas of the home.

| Area of the home | Type of insulation |
|---|---|
| Attic | |
| Hot water cylinder | |
| Walls | |
| Windows | |

| 8 |

19. What is the purpose of a Building Energy Rating certificate?

_____

_____

| 2 |

20. Why is good ventilation important in the home?

_____

_____

_____

| 4 |

21. Suggest **two** methods of ventilation suitable for the kitchen.

    (i) _____  (ii) _____  | 2 |

22. (i) What is condensation?

    _____

    _____  | 2 |

    (ii) What problems can condensation cause in the home?

    _____

    _____  | 4 |

    (iii) How can condensation be controlled?

    _____

    _____  | 4 |

23. Suggest **six** ways to conserve energy in the home.

    (i) _____

    (ii) _____

    (iii) _____

    (iv) _____

    (v) _____  | 6 |

    (vi) _____

Total / Mark

**Homework Assignment 44**

| 108 |

*Teacher's comment*

_____

Date of issue             Due date

This topic comes up frequently at both **Higher** and **Ordinary Level** as a long question: **HL 2009** (fridge), **2007** (microwave), **2003** (cooker), **2002** (fridge), **2000** (microwave), **1996** (cooker), **1994** (fridge); **OL 2009** (cooker), **2005** (fridge), **2001** (cooker), **1997** (cooker), **1995** (fridge).

On years where it has not come up as a long question, it is usually asked in the short questions instead. There have only been a few years where it was not asked for at all: **HL 2004, 2004, 1997, 1995; OL 2009, 2008, 2004, 2003, 2000.**

1. Classify the following electrical appliances according to whether they have a motor, an element or both.

> kettle, washing machine, deep fat fryer, toaster,
> vacuum cleaner, electric knife, food processor, cooker, fridge,
> dishwasher, fan, sandwich toaster

| Motor | Element | Both |
| --- | --- | --- |
| | | |

12

## Microwave

2. List the guidelines to be considered when choosing a microwave cooker for a modern kitchen.

_____

_____

_____ 

_____  8

3. Give three advantages of using a microwave cooker.

(i) _____

(ii) _____

(iii) _____  6

4. Give three disadvantages of using a microwave cooker.

(i) _____

(ii) _____

(iii) _____  6

5. Suggest three different uses for a microwave cooker.

(i) _____

(ii) _____

(iii) _____  6

6. Name two materials suitable for microwave cookware/dishes.

(i) _____

(ii) _____  2

7.  List the rules that should be followed when using and cleaning a microwave cooker.

    (i)  Using: _____

    _____

    _____

    _____ [4]

    (ii)  Cleaning: _____

    _____

    _____

    _____ [4]

8.  Explain the term 'standing time'.

    _____ [2]


## Cooker

9.  State the main advantage of cooking by gas, cooking by electricity and cooking by solid fuel.

    (i)  Gas: _____

    (ii)  Electricity: _____

    (iii)  Solid fuel: _____ [6]

10.  Which type of cooker would you buy for your own home? Give two reasons for your choice.

    (i)  Choice: _____

    (ii)  Reasons: _____

    _____ [4]

11. List four modern features of modern cookers and suggest one advantage of each feature.

| Feature | Advantage |
|---|---|
| (i) | |
| (ii) | |
| (iii) | |
| (iv) | |

8

12. Give three guidelines to be followed when positioning a cooker in the kitchen.

(i) _____

(ii) _____

(iii) _____

6

13. Suggest three ways to save energy when cooking.

(i) _____

(ii) _____

(iii) _____

6

14. Describe how you should clean a cooker.

_____

_____

_____

_____

_____

_____

_____

10

15. Why is good ventilation necessary when cooking?

_____  _____

## Refrigerator

16. Bearing in mind the need to protect the environment, write a note on refrigerators under each of the following headings.

    (i)   Choice: _____

    _____

    _____

    (ii)  Use: _____

    _____

    _____

    (iii) Care and cleaning: _____

    _____

    _____

    (iv)  Disposal: _____

    _____

    _____

17. Name and give the function of three modern refrigerator features.

| Name | Function |
| --- | --- |
| (i) | |
| (ii) | |
| (iii) | |

18. Discuss the importance of temperature control in a refrigerator.

_____

_____

_____ 4

19. What does the EU Directive on Waste Electrical and Electronic Equipment 2005 mean for the consumer?

_____

_____ 2

Total Mark

**Homework Assignment 45**

120

_Teacher's comment_

Date of issue                                        Due date

This topic has come up every four or five years at **Higher Level** as a long question. The usual two topics are home hygiene and safety and first aid: **HL 2005** (fire safety and first aid), **2001** (home hygiene), **1995** (fire safety and first aid). The topic also comes up at **Ordinary Level**: **2008** (home hygiene), **2004** (home hygiene), **2003** (fire safety and first aid), **1999** (accident prevention and first aid). This section also features in the short questions at both levels:

**HL**   **2008, 2001, 2000, 1997, 1995**

**OL**   **2009, 2007, 2006, 2001.**

1.  A clean, hygienic home contributes to healthy living. Give four guidelines necessary to ensure a high standard of hygiene in the home.

    (i) _____

    (ii) _____

    (iii) _____

    (iv) _____

    | 8 |

2.  Give two possible consequences of poor hygiene in the home.

    (i) _____

    (ii) _____

    | 4 |

3.  Plan a simple daily routine that would help a teenager with asthma to maintain a high standard of hygiene in his or her bedroom.

_____

_____

_____

_____

_____

_____ | 6 |

4.  Give a different use for **each** of the following cleaning agents.

| Cleaning agent | Use |
|---|---|
| (i)    Detergent | |
| (ii)   Bleach | |
| (iii)  Cream cleaner | |
| (iv)   Disinfectant | |
| (v)    Wax polish | |

| 10 |

5.  List four safety guidelines that should be followed when storing and using household cleaning agents.

(i)   _____

(ii)  _____

(iii) _____

(iv)  _____ | 4 |

6. Sketch one hazard symbol to convey to the consumer that the product is either highly flammable, toxic or a harmful irritant.

2

7. List four common causes of accidents in the home.

(i) _____

(ii) _____

(iii) _____

(iv) _____

4

8. List the safety guidelines that should be followed in order to prevent fire in the home.

_____

_____

_____

_____

8

9. In the event of a household fire, give three points of procedure to follow to ensure the safety of the occupants of the house.

(i) _____

(ii) _____

(iii) _____

6

10. Name two different pieces of fire safety equipment suitable for use in the home.

(i) _____ (ii) _____

2

11. Describe the first aid treatment for a major burn or scald.

_____

_____ | 2 |

12. Explain why water should **not** be used to extinguish a fire caused by an electrical fault or a fat fire.

    (i)   Electrical fault: _____ | 2 |

    (ii)  Fat fire: _____ | 2 |

13. What are the **three** aims of first aid?

    (i)   _____

    (ii)  _____

    (iii) _____ | 6 |

14. Name **six** items you would expect to find in a first aid box.

    (i)   _____    (ii)  _____

    (iii) _____    (iv) _____

    (v)  _____    (vi) _____ | 6 |

15. Briefly describe the first aid treatment for each of the following.

(i) A minor burn or scald: _____ _____

_____ _____ | 2 |

(ii) A minor cut: _____ _____ _____

_____ | 2 |

(iii) An adult that appears to be choking: _____ _____

_____ | 2 |

(iv) A child that appears to be choking: _____ _____

_____ | 2 |

(v) A child who has swallowed tablets: _____ _____

_____ | 2 |

Total / Mark

**Homework Assignment 46**

*Teacher's comment*

**82**

**Chapter 30**      Community Services and the Environment

Date of issue                                    Due date

This topic comes up almost every year at **Higher Level**. However, it has not come up as a full long question to date (**2009**). It is more likely to come up as a short question or one part of a long question. At **Ordinary Level**, the environment as a topic has come up as a long question twice (**2007, 2000**). It features regularly (although not always) in the short questions (**2007, 2006, 2004, 2003, 1999, 1998, 1997**).

1.   What is meant by environmental pollution?

_____

_____    | 2 |

2.   Describe four ways the environment is being polluted.

(i)   _____

(ii)  _____

(iii) _____

(iv)  _____    | 8 |

3.   Define climate change.

_____

_____    | 2 |

4.   What are the main negative effects of climate change?

_____

_____    | 6 |

5. List four different reasons for an increase of greenhouse gases.

(i) _____

(ii) _____

(iii) _____

(iv) _____          [ 4 ]


6. (i) What is the ozone layer?

_____

_____          [ 2 ]

(ii) What is the function of the ozone layer? What is the main negative effect of its depletion?

(a) Function: _____

(b) Effect of depletion: _____          [ 4 ]

(iii) Suggest two ways the ozone layer can be protected.

(a) _____

(b) _____          [ 4 ]


7. (i) Describe two causes of water pollution in Ireland.

(a) _____

(b) _____          [ 4 ]

(ii) List two effects of water pollution.

(a) _____

(b) _____          [ 4 ]

(iii) Suggest **four** ways the consumer could reduce water consumption in the home.

(a) _____

(b) _____

(c) _____

(d) _____  8

8. Explain the term 'biodegradable waste'.

_____  2

9. Tick whether **each** of the following are organic waste **or** inorganic waste.

| Waste | Organic | Inorganic |
|---|---|---|
| (i) Potato peelings | | |
| (ii) Food cans | | |
| (iii) Glass bottles | | |
| (iv) Food scraps | | |
| (v) Plastic bags | | |
| (vi) Cereal boxes | | |

12

10. Suggest **four** ways the consumer can reduce the amount of household waste produced.

(i) _____

(ii) _____

(iii) _____

(iv) _____  4

11. In waste management, suggest a **different** method of disposing of **each** of the following waste items.

　　(i)　Vegetable peelings: _____

　　(ii)　Clothes: _____

　　(iii)　Coloured glass: _____　| 6 |

12. What information does this symbol convey to the consumer?

_____
_____　| 2 |

13. List **four** household items that can be recycled.

　　(i)　_____　(ii)　_____

　　(iii)　_____　(iv)　_____　| 4 |

14. Describe **four** ways consumers can help protect the environment.

　　(i)　_____

　　(ii)　_____

　　(iii)　_____

　　(iv)　_____　| 8 |

15. Describe three different actions taken by the Irish government in recent times to help protect the environment.

   (i) _____

   _____

   (ii) _____

   _____

   (iii) _____    6

   _____

16. Name two organisations concerned with environmental protection.    2

   (i) _____    (ii) _____

17. What are statutory services? Name two statutory services provided in your area.    2

   (i) What they are: _____

   (ii) Examples: _____    _____    2

18. What are local amenities? Name two amenities found in your area.    2

   (i) What they are: _____

   (ii) Examples: _____    _____    2

Total Mark

**Homework Assignment 47**

**102**

*Teacher's comment*

_____

# Unit 5

# Textile Studies

Date of issue                                    Due date

This topic does not come up very often at **Higher Level**. It has only appeared twice as a long question (**2009** and **2003**) and in **2005**, **1998**, **1997** and **1994** as a short question. At **Ordinary Level**, this topic has come up as part of a long question on three occasions: **2007** (curtains), **2005 and 2001** (as part of a long question on making a household item). In the short questions, students are frequently asked for the functions of curtains (**2009**, **2006**, **2002**, **1996**).

1.  List four different uses for textiles in the home.

    (i) _____

    (ii) _____

    (iii) _____

    (iv) _____    | 8 |

2.  Suggest two desirable properties for **each** of the following household items.

| Household item | Two desirable properties |
|---|---|
| (i)   Bed sheets | |
| (ii)  Carpets | |
| (iii) Duvet | |
| (iv)  Upholstery fabric | |

| 8 |

3.  Describe three factors that should be considered when choosing soft
    furnishings for the home.

    (i)   _____

    (ii)  _____

    (iii) _____                    6


4.  Give one advantage and one disadvantage of making soft furnishings for
    the home as opposed to shop bought.

    (i)   Advantage: _____

    (ii)  Disadvantage: _____                    4


5.  Give four functions of curtains.

    (i)   _____

    (ii)  _____

    (iii) _____

    (iv)  _____                     4


6.  List three desirable properties of textiles suitable for curtains.

    (i)   _____      (ii) _____

    (iii) _____                                               6


7.  Name two fabrics suitable for curtains and one reason for your choice in
    each case.

    (i)   Curtain fabric 1: _____

          Reason for choice: _____

    (ii)  Curtain fabric 2: _____                    8

          Reason for choice: _____

8. Name two soft furnishings other than curtains that you would consider suitable for a living room.

(i) _____    (ii) _____    | 4 |

Homework Assignment 48

48

*Teacher's comment*

**49**

**Chapter 32**    Clothing, Fashion and Design

Date of issue                                    Due date

This topic comes up almost every year as a short question at **Higher Level**, but to date has only come up once as a long question (2004), when it was part of a question on the item of clothing made by students in practical class. At **Ordinary Level**, this topic comes up frequently as a long question, but like at Higher Level, as part of a question on making a simple item of clothing.

1.  Describe four functions of clothing.

    (i) _____

    (ii) _____

    (iii) _____

    (iv) _____     | 8 |

2.  What are fashion trends? Give two examples of current fashion trends.

    (i)  What they are: _____     | 2 |

    (ii) Examples: _____     | 2 |

3.  Describe four factors that influence fashion trends.

    (i) _____

    (ii) _____

    (iii) _____

    (iv) _____     | 8 |

4.  Explain the following terms in relation to clothing.

    (i)  Haute couture: _____

    _____

    (ii)  Prêt-a-porter: _____

    _____

    8 / 8

5.  Describe **three** factors that frequently influence people's choice of clothing.

    (i)  _____

    (ii)  _____

    (iii)  _____

    6

6.  List **four** guidelines that should be considered before buying clothing.

    (i)  _____

    (ii)  _____

    (iii)  _____

    (iv)  _____

    8

7.  Explain how **each** of the following can affect the appearance of a garment.

    (i)  Vertical lines: _____

    (ii)  Horizontal lines: _____

    4

8.  Give **two** examples of accessories.

    (i)  _____  (ii)  _____

    2

Total Mark

**Homework Assignment 49**

48

*Teacher's comment*

_____

## Chapter 33     Fibres and Fabrics

Date of issue                  Due date

This topic comes up almost every year at **Higher Level** in the short questions.
In addition, it is a popular long question (**2009, 2008, 2005, 2002, 1997**).
As a long question, students are often asked in detail about a particular fibre,
e.g. wool (**2005**), silk (**2008**), cotton (**2002**).

At **Ordinary Level**, this topic does feature most years as a short question
(usually asked to identify wool symbol, classify fibres and fabric finishes).
The topic has only come up once as part of a long question, in 2003.

1.   (i)   Tick whether **each** of the following is natural or man-made.

| Fabric | Natural | Man-made |
|---|---|---|
| (a)   Cotton | | |
| (b)   Linen | | |
| (c)   Nylon | | |
| (d)   Polyester | | |
| (e)   Rayon | | |
| (f)   Silk | | |
| (g)   Viscose | | |
| (h)   Wool | | |

8

  (ii)   Which two fibres from the list above are synthetic?

(a) _____     (b) _____

2

2. Wool is a popular natural fibre.

   (i) Give two other examples of natural fibres.

   (a) _____   (b) _____   | 2 |

   (ii) Name two types of wool fabric.

   (a) _____   (b) _____   | 2 |

   (iii) Sketch a care label suitable for a wool jumper (see Chapter 34).

   | 4 |

   (iv) Describe a fabric test that could be carried out in order to identify wool.

   _____

   _____

   _____

   _____   | 4 |

3. (i) Outline the stages in silk production.

   _____

   _____

   _____   | 4 / 4 |

   _____

   (ii) State three desirable and three undesirable properties of silk.

   | Desirable | Undesirable |
   |---|---|
   |  |  |
   |  |  |
   |  |  |

   | 6 / 6 |

(iii) Name two different types of silk fabric.

(a) _____ (b) _____ [2]

(iv) Name two household items that could be made from silk.

(a) _____ (b) _____ [2]

4. Cotton is a versatile and popular textile.
   (i) Outline the stages involved in the production of cotton. _____

   _____

   _____

   _____ [4]

   (ii) List four different examples of cotton fabric.

   (a) _____ (b) _____

   (c) _____ (d) _____ [4]

   (iii) State two desirable and two undesirable properties of cotton.

| Desirable | Undesirable |
|---|---|
|  |  |

[4]

   (iv) Suggest two fabric finishes that could be applied to cotton and explain why they would be of benefit.

   (a) Fabric finish: _____

   Why? _____

   (b) Fabric finish: _____

   Why? _____ [8]

   (v) Sketch a symbol that indicates that a fabric is pure cotton.

[4]

5. Linen is a textile traditionally produced in Ireland.

   (i) Outline the stages involved in the production of linen.

   _____

   _____

   _____

   _____ | 4 |

   (ii) List two different examples of linen fabric.

   (a) _____ (b) _____ | 2 |

   (iii) State two desirable and two undesirable properties of linen.

   | Desirable | Undesirable |
   | --- | --- |
   | | |
   | | | | 4 |

   (iv) Suggest two fabric finishes that could be applied to linen and explain why they would be of benefit.

   (a) Fabric finish: _____

      Why? _____

   (b) Fabric finish: _____

      Why? _____ | 8 |

   (v) Sketch a symbol that indicates that a fabric is pure linen.

   +-----------+
   |           |
   |           |
   |           |
   +-----------+                                      | 4 |

6.  (i)  Name two regenerated fabrics.

        (a) _____    (b) ___ _____    2

    (ii) Explain how regenerated fabrics are produced.

        _____    _____

        _____

        _____

        _____

        _____    6

        _____

    (iii) State two desirable and two undesirable properties of regenerated fabrics.

        | Desirable | Undesirable |
        | --- | --- |
        |  |  |
        |  |  |    4

    (iv) Give two different uses of regenerated fabrics.

        (a) _____    (b) _____    4


7.  (i)  Name three synthetic fabrics and give one example of where **each** one
         is used.

        (a) Fabric 1: _____

            Use: _____

        (b) Fabric 2: _____

            Use: _____

        (c) Fabric 3: _____

            Use: _____    6

(ii) Explain how synthetic fabrics are produced.

_____

_____

_____

_____ | 6 |

_____

(iii) State two desirable and two undesirable properties of synthetic fabrics.

| Desirable | Undesirable |
|-----------|-------------|
|           |             | 4

8. What do these two symbols indicate to the consumer?

WOOLMARK

WOOL BLEND

(i) _____ (ii) _____ | 4 |

9. Name two different ways that yarn can be made into fabric.

(i) _____ (ii) _____ | 4 |

10. What are bonded fabrics? Give one example of a bonded fabric.

(i) Bonded fabrics are: _____

(ii) Example: _____ | 4 |

11. Explain the following terms.

(i) Ply: _____

(ii) Denier: _____ | 4 |

12. (i) Complete the table below by matching each of the fabric finishes with the purpose for which it has been applied.

flame-resistant, anti-static, brushed, crease-resistant

| Purpose | Fabric finish |
|---|---|
| Prevents fabric clinging to the body | |
| Makes fabric burn less easily | |
| Reduces the need to iron fabric | |
| Makes fabric feel softer and warmer | |

8

(ii) Name a fabric that would benefit from the following fabric finishes. Explain your choice in each case.

(a) Anti-static: _____

Why? _____  2

(b) Flame-resistant: _____

Why? _____  2

(c) Crease-resistant: _____

Why? _____  2

(d) Moth-proofing: _____

Why? _____  2

13. Suggest two ways pattern can be added to fabric.

(i) _____  (ii) _____  4

14. Burning tests can be used to identify fibres and fabrics. Complete the table below to demonstrate how various fibres and fabrics react to this test.

| Fibre(s) | Odour | How it burns | Residue |
|---|---|---|---|
| Wool or silk | Burning hair | | |
| Cotton, linen, viscose | | Quickly | Paper-like ash |
| | Celery | Melts | |

10

# 51

Chapter 34    Fabric Care

Date of issue                                Due date

This topic has come up almost every year to date at **Higher Level**, usually as a short question or one part of a long question. For both levels, students need to be able to recognise fabric care symbols, design care labels for common fabrics (wool, silk) and know how to treat common stains.

1.  How should clothes be cared for before storing?

_____

_____

_____

4

2.  Explain what **each** of the following symbols indicate.

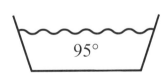        

(i) _____       (ii) _____ 95°       (iii) _____

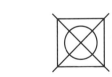        

(iv) _____       (v) _____       (vi) _____

(vii) _____       (viii) _____

8

3. How should clothing be prepared for machine washing?

_____

_____

_____

_____  | 8 |

4. List **four** guidelines to be followed when washing a delicate item of clothing.

(i) _____

(ii) _____

(iii) _____

(iv) _____  | 8 |

5. What does the term 'colourfast' mean?

_____  | 2 |

6. Describe how you would remove the following stains from clothing.

(i) Tea: _____  | 2 |

(ii) Chewing gum: _____  | 2 |

(iii) Grass: _____  | 2 |

(iv) Chocolate: _____  | 2 |

(v) Mildew: _____  | 2 |

7. What precautions should be taken when using commercial stain removers?

_____  | 2 |

8. Clothing detergents contain a number of active ingredients, each with a different function. What is the function of **each** of the following detergent ingredients?

    (i)   Emulsifiers: _____ | 2 |

_____

    (ii)  Bleach: _____ | 2 |

    (iii) Enzymes: _____ | 2 |

    (iv) Water softener: _____ | 2 |

    (v)  Perfume: _____ | 2 |

9. Write out this care label in words.

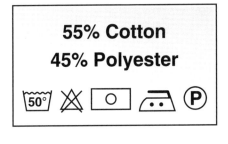

_____

_____ | 5 |

10. Design a care label for the household item or item of clothing you made as part of this course.

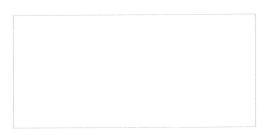

| 5 |

11. Draw a care label for each of the following.

   (i)   Wool jumper

   (ii)  Silk blouse

   (iii) Pair of jeans

   (iv)  100% polyester football shirt

   8

12. What is the purpose of fabric conditioner and biological detergent?

   (i)   Fabric conditioner: _____

   (ii)  Biological detergent: _____

   4

Total Mark

**Homework Assignment 51**

74

*Teacher's comment*

| Chapter 35 | Needlework Skills |
|---|---|

Date of issue                                         Due date

This topic comes up almost every year at both levels in the short questions. When this topic comes up as a long question, it is usually about the sewing machine.

1. Outline **five** general guidelines for hand sewing.

   (i) _____

   (ii) _____

   (iii) _____

   (iv) _____

   (v) _____

   10

2. List **six** pieces of essential sewing equipment.

   (i) _____

   (ii) _____

   (iii) _____

   (iv) _____

   (v) _____

   (vi) _____

   6

3.  Name **each** of the following hand stitches and suggest **one** use for each.

(i)

Name of stitch: _____

Use: _____

_____

(ii)

Name of stitch: _____

Use: _____

_____

(iii)

Name of stitch: _____

Use: _____

_____

(iv)

Name of stitch: _____

Use: _____

_____

(v)

Name of stitch: _____

Use: _____

_____

(vi)

Name of stitch: _____

Use: _____

_____

(vii)

Name of stitch: _____

Use: _____

_____

(viii)

Name of stitch: _____

Use: _____

_____

(ix)

Name of stitch: _____

Use: _____

_____

(x)

Name of stitch: _____

Use: _____

_____

20

4. (i) Name the parts of the sewing machine labelled 1 to 6.

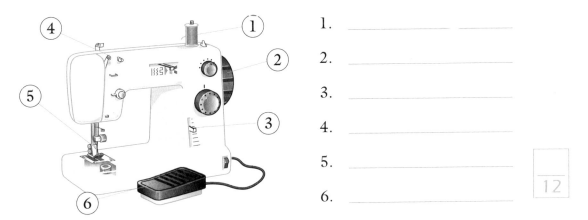

1. _____

2. _____

3. _____

4. _____

5. _____

6. _____

[12]

(ii) List the guidelines that should be followed when choosing, using **and** caring for a sewing machine.

(a) Choosing: _____

_____

_____

[4]

(b) Using: _____

_____

_____

[4]

(c) Caring: _____

_____

_____

[4]

(iii) Give **one** reason for **each** of the following machine faults.

(a) Needle breaking: _____ [2]

(b) Looped stitches: _____ [2]

(c) Thread breaking: _____ [2]

(iv) Suggest a different machine stitch for each of the following.

    (a) Appliqué: _____

    (b) Turning up a hem: _____ | 4 |

5. Name the seam pictured here and suggest **three** different ways its raw edges could be neatened.

    (i) Name of seam: _____

    (ii) Three neatening methods:

        (a) _____ (b) _____ (c) _____ | 8 |

6. Explain each of the following terms.

    (i) Nap: _____ | 2 |

    (ii) Straight grain: _____ | 2 |

    (iii) Bias: _____ | 2 |

    (iv) Selvedge: _____ | 2 |

7. What do the following **two** pattern markings indicate?

    _____

    _____ | 4 |

8. Suggest **two** methods of transferring pattern markings to fabric.

    (i) _____ (ii) _____ | 4 |

Total Mark

**Homework Assignment 52**

| **94** |

*Teacher's comment*

# 53

| Chapter 36 | Practical Needlework Tasks |
|---|---|

Date of issue                                    Due date

This topic comes up every number of years in section B, question 5 at both levels. The type of information asked at each level is quite different, so they will be dealt with separately here. To complete this question well in the exam, you will also need to have a good knowledge of two other chapters as well – fabric care (Chapter 34) and needlework skills (Chapter 35).

## Higher Level

### HL  2007, 2004, 2000

1. Your class has been asked to make a set of aprons for use in your home economics class. Name the fabric you would choose for the aprons and give three reasons for your choice.

   (i)   Choice of fabric: _____

   (ii)  Reasons for choice:

      (a)  _____

      (b)  _____

      (c)  _____     8

2. List the guidelines to be considered when buying the fabric.

   (i)    _____

   (ii)   _____

   (iii)  _____

   (iv)   _____     4

3. Sketch and describe the apron you would make.

   (i) Sketch:

   6

   (ii) Description: _____

   _____

   _____

   6

4. Suggest two ways your class could personalise the aprons for your class.

   (i) _____

   (ii) _____

   4

5. Sketch and describe a suitable care label for the aprons you have made.

   (i) Sketch:

   (ii) Description: _____

   _____

   8

Total Mark

**Homework Assignment 53 (Higher Level)**

**36**

*Teacher's comment*

_____

**OL  2009, 2005, 2002, 2001, 1998, 1997, 1996**

At **Ordinary Level**, students are usually asked about either (a) the item of clothing or (b) household item that they made as part of their practical sewing work.

1.  Give three uses of textiles in the home.

    (i) _____

    (ii) _____

    (iii) _____

    6

2.  Name, sketch and describe a household item you have made as part of your textile studies.

    (i)  Name: _____

    (ii) Description: _____

    _____

    _____

    _____

    _____

    _____

    _____

    6

3.  Name the fabric(s) you used to make the household item.

    _____

    _____

    2

4. List three points you considered when choosing fabric(s) for the household item.

   (i) _____

   (ii) _____

   (iii) _____

   6

5. Describe a decorative feature suitable for the item you have made.

   _____

   _____

   4

6. Name, sketch and describe the garment you have made as part of your textile studies.

   (i) Name: _____

   (ii) Description: _____

   _____

   _____

   _____

   _____

   _____

   6

7. Name the fabric(s) you used to make the garment.

   _____

   _____

   2

8. List three points you considered when choosing fabric(s) for the garment.

(i) _____

(ii) _____

(iii) _____ 6

9. In addition to the fabric, list six items you required in order to make up and finish the garment.

(i) _____ (ii) _____

(iii) _____ (iv) _____

(v) _____ (vi) _____ 6

10. Give two examples of stitches you used when making up the garment.

(i) _____ (ii) _____ 4

Total / Mark

**Homework Assignment 53  (Ordinary Level)**

48

*Teacher's comment*

_____

For permission to reproduce photographs the author and publisher gratefully acknowledge the following:

© Alamy: 106, 116 (vi), 116 (viii), 116 (ix), 146; © Getty: 170, 175; Courtesy of Australian Wool Innovation: 188L, 188R; Courtesy of British Standards Institution: 116 (v); Courtesy of Coeliac UK: 30; Courtesy of Excellence Ireland Quality Association: 116 (i); Courtesy of Guaranteed Irish: 116 (ii); Courtesy of NSAI: 116 (iii); Courtesy of State Examinations Commission: 87; Courtesy of Wikimedia Commons: 116 (vii).

The author and publisher have made every effort to trace all copyright holders, but if any has been inadvertently overlooked we would be pleased to make the necessary arrangement at the first opportunity.